Multiply Your Profits

Multiply Your Profits

A Common-Sense Approach for Small to Midsize Businesses

Richard Peelo

Inverness Publishers, Inc.
Inverness, Illinois

Multiply Your Profits
A Common-Sense Approach for Small to Midsize Businesses
Richard Peelo

Library of Congress Cataloging-in-Publication Data

Peelo, Richard, 1941–
Multiply your profits: a common-sense approach for small to midsize businesses / Richard Peelo.
p. cm.
Includes index.
ISBN 0-9661609-0-8 (hardcover: alk. paper)
1. Small business—Finance. 2. Corporate profits. 3. Industrial management. I. Title.
HG4027.7.P44 1998
658.15'92—dc21 97-46410
CIP

10 9 8 7 6 5 4 3 2 1

ISBN: 0-9661609-0-8

Printed in the United States of America

Printed on acid-free paper

Published by: Inverness Publishers, Inc.
137 South Roberts
Inverness, IL 60067
Phone 847-202-1500 Fax 847-202-1502
E-mail InvernPub@aol.com

To my mother and father, the best parents
ever created.

To Jill, a.k.a. "Pumkins."

To David, Heather, Lisa, and Jessica,
the joys of my life.

Contents

Preface: Why You Should Read This Book xi

1 Hiring Smart People 1
Add an ACE to Your Staff............................ 3
Corporate Culture 4
How Do You Manage Them? 5
Leadership.. 8
Effective Leaders................................... 9
Summary 12

2 Every Dollar of Expense Is One Less Dollar of Profit... 13
Sacred Cows... 16
Excessive (Nonproductive) Staff..................... 17
Sales Commissions 19
How to Manage Expenses.............................. 20
Organizational Analysis 21
Ratio Analysis 22
Quality 27
Purchasing.. 29
Your Expenses 32

3 Cash Flow Is the Name of the Game 37
Fast Growth Corporation 39
Cash Flow Formula 48
Credit Management 49
Lost Revenue 54
Inventory 55
More Suggestions to Improve Cash Flow 60
Troubled Businesses 60
Summary 61

4 Price Right to Profit 63
Setting Your Prices 66
Break-Even Analysis 69
Sales Volume and Price Changes 69
Product Line Profit Picture 79
Incremental Cost Pricing 82
One-Price Policy Versus a Varying Price Policy 83
Summary 83

5 Each Customer Is an Annuity 85
Why Poor Service Costs You 90
Superb Customer Service 91
How to Deliver Superb Service 93
Employee Satisfaction and Customer Satisfaction Go Together 93
Customer Feedback 96
Some Final Thoughts 98
Summary 99

6 Business Planning.. 101
What Is a Business Plan? 104
How to Proceed 104
Follow-Through... 110
Why Business Plans Fail 111
Future Periods 111
Summary 112

7 Good Management Makes the Difference........... 113
The "Intangible" Balance Sheet 114
How Businesses Prosper....................................... 117
"What Went Wrong?"... 119
Management Information Systems to Monitor Key Indicators.... 127
Innovate, Not Imitate.. 131
Conclusion... 133

Appendix: Profit Patrol...................................... 135

Index.. 147

About the Author 155

Preface: Why You Should Read This Book

The fact is that many seemingly profitable businesses are not as profitable as they should be, mainly due to shortcomings in their business practices. Many waste money on activities that add little to the business while paying little heed to those that could truly make a difference and could significantly multiply profits in the process.

You may be saying to yourself that with some changes, increasing profits by 20% or perhaps even 40% may be possible. I believe that doubling or tripling your profits might be a conservative estimate. Perhaps they can be multiplied four, five, or even 10 times.

This book does not offer five or 10 easy steps to multiply your profits. A quick fix such as an expense cut or price increase can deliver an increase in profits, but multiplying your profits is much more than this. It involves a whole host of factors that, when brought together, yield the optimum profit. You must:

- Delight and retain your customers, for each is an annuity, providing a continuous and growing stream of revenue that translates into profits.
- Manage and develop your "intangible" assets, for they are the real assets of the business that will enable you to keep multiplying your profits in the years ahead.

- Invest and manage for the long term.
- Manage your finances effectively to yield the greatest profit flow from the capital available.
- Know how to set prices.
- Plan. Know where you are going. Have a vision and a clear strategy for your business.
- Eliminate non–revenue-producing expenditures.
- Put in place a control system that monitors your key indicators.
- Learn the secrets of successful businesses and why they continue to multiply their profits.
- Learn why some businesses are unsuccessful, and how you can avoid falling into that condition.
- Hire the smartest people—proven winners. Then give them the ball and let them run with it.

The sum of all these efforts will multiply your profits, leading to optimum profitability.

Wishful thinking is not going to produce results. Only a total commitment on your part and on the part of your staff to a specific program for multiplying your profits, will get you there. The journey may not always be easy, but the results and ensuing self-satisfaction from pursuing a worthwhile endeavor will more than compensate for the effort.

The appendix is entitled "Profit Patrol." It serves as a checkup on the health of your business and your current efforts to achieve its optimum profitability. It includes a comprehensive series of questions that cover the primary points made in this book—a form of self-audit. Completing it should enable you to identify your weak points that you can then focus on for rectification and enhanced profits.

Go to it. The results will be worth the effort.

1 Hiring Smart People

I hired a lot of smart people.

—Bill Gates

The secret to your success is people. For it is they who

- Energize your business.
- Innovate.
- Convert your goals into productivity.
- Delight customers.
- Determine whether you make a profit or a loss.

Good people, well trained and motivated, can make a huge difference to your bottom line. They are the single most important resource in any business. Thus, selecting the right people is a vital step to business success and profits.

A simple rule is:

Hire the very best people!

Pay them every penny that they are worth, and more!

Then, get out of their way! Provide the resources and let them do the job you hired them for.

You don't tell a .400 hitter in baseball how to hold the bat.

As a businessperson, the most important decision you make is the people you hire. They are also your biggest investment. So it makes sense to take care of them—their morale, their skills, their participation, and their paychecks.

You build a business by building your people. Their personal growth is the thrust for the business's growth. In the end, your most important sustainable resource is the quality of your people.

Most people are like mirrors. They reflect back what they are given. Take care of them, and they'll take care of you and your company. As Denis Connor, the successful America's Cup yachtsman, said: "I surrounded myself with quality people that made me look good." Winners know that they are winners, and they surround themselves with other winners. They don't need any yes-men around to boost their ego. Winners know that they will achieve much more with the right people in place. Being brilliant can be a disadvantage, because you think you can do it all yourself. So unless you know it all yourself, you need to surround yourself with smart people. Bring in people more talented than you are.

Consider the phenomenal success achieved by three men who started with little in monetary terms, but were extremely careful in whom they chose to work with them: Bill Gates, Ross Perot, and Sam Walton. Each of these gentlemen became billionaires a number of times over, in good part because of their ability to choose and lead the right people. Each recognized this: Do right by your people, and they'll do right by you. Give them a company to be proud of; take care of them, and they'll put forth their best effort for you. As Napoleon said, "Morale is the soul of victory."

Another factor concerning these men, not always recognized by many, is that they have always had a very strong affinity and liking for others, and genuinely cared abut the well-being and success of all their people, not just a chosen few. Businesses that are people-oriented outperform their competition by staggering margins.

ADD AN ACE TO YOUR STAFF

Remember that talent has no pattern. I suggest that you look for people who have a history of success; people who like to compete and win and are driven to be the best; people with good judgment and common sense. Seek out assertive and creative people who push new ideas and challenge historical rationales. As Ross Perot said, "Eagles don't flock; they fly one at a time." All businesses need to be refreshed with new ideas and new approaches.

When it comes time to hire, add an ACE to your staff. How do you know who is an ACE? By applying the ACE test:

A = Attitude

C = Character

E = Enthusiasm

A person with these three attributes is pretty much a certain winner. The right attitude, supported by enthusiasm and integrity, will overcome nearly every obstacle. Look for these qualities when making your hiring decisions.

Without all three of these qualities, a person will not make it. And don't assume that enthusiasm only applies to extroverts. Some of your most enthusiastic workers just might brilliantly carry forth their responsibilities quietly and professionally. Two other qualities are equally important to achieving success; namely, persistence and determination.

Think about it, and choose your people as carefully as a top-flight National Football League coach chooses his players. And just as a team with raw rookies and seasoned players, all the talent in the world won't transform them into a winning club unless your training and system of doing business is in order. But without the talented people, even the best system will not produce the desired results.

A word of warning before we go on: People invariably hire others who mirror themselves or who are not a threat to themselves or their position. Outgoing people gravitate toward others who are extroverts. Introverts are more comfortable with other introverts. Self-confident people prefer the company of those with the same disposition. Those lacking self-confidence will often not choose self-confident, outgoing types who are likely to question and rock the boat. Autocratic types prefer yes-men.

Do not be afraid to hire a person with a different vision, a non-conformism or free thinker, and people who break the mold—for they see a different way of doing things. They are free spirits. All businesses need their creative, innovative thinking. Conformists will often not hire such people, because they are so different than themselves. This is a problem. Many of history's greatest leaders had a different way of looking at things, a different vision.

So many of our greatest sports stars similarly fall into this category. Not only do they have great talent, but they pursue a level of excellence uncommon in their field.

I suggest that you be aware of what category you fit into, and be mindful not to choose a person based solely on personal compatibility. Second, I suggest that you honestly and candidly assess the qualities and talents required to fill the position. What depth of experience and knowledge is required?

Only after a full assessment of all factors should a hiring decision be made. The people you hire will determine whether you are successful. Hire a motivated and intelligent person, and you have an opportunity to grow. Hire an individual unsuited for the position, and you will go backwards.

CORPORATE CULTURE

And now, a second word of caution. No matter how talented, enthusiastic, and experienced your employees are, a poor corporate culture and structure can stifle their best ideals. A company's culture and its performance are deeply linked.

What is a business's culture? It has been said that a business's culture is its "personality." It is a combination of its behaviors, assumptions, thoughts, values, and symbols that are developed over time.

The organization's culture can have a pronounced effect on its success. The more the culture broadens the freedom of the employees, the more likely it is that the business will succeed. When a business values freedom, employee diversity, teamwork, and flexibility, its prospects are enhanced. Employees need the freedom to express themselves and to display their creativity. That freedom helps foster productivity and quality. When people feel comfortable, they work smarter and more productively.

An autocratic culture, or "one-man rule," stifles all creativity and initiative. The freedom to offer suggestions or constructive criticism, or to express opinions, is vital to employee satisfaction. It's the only way for a company to attract smart people and keep them motivated. And, within reason, you must allow them to make some mistakes. Without these aspects of a company's culture, inferior work habits and inferior products become inevitable.

What is your company's culture? How do you propose to improve it? Don't be defensive, for nobody is perfect. Are you an autocratic ruler? The odds are that this describes you. A small dose of honest introspection here might prove very worthwhile.

HOW DO YOU MANAGE THEM?

You have a talented, loyal, enthusiastic staff in place. How do you manage them? Here are some suggestions.

- Help them achieve their hopes and dreams, in the same way that you want them to help you achieve yours. When their needs are being satisfied, they will doubly make sure that yours are too.

- Hiring talented people builds a foundation of steel, so you need to create the environment/culture for your people to grow and exercise their initiative. Provide responsibility and give them freedom to act along with it. Challenge them. Always ask, "How can we improve this?" or "How can we do better?" Make sure it is safe for them to take chances. When you raise up able subordinates, they attract others of their kind. It is said of the great basketball star, Michael Jordan, that he validates his greatness by his ability to help elevate the level of play of his teammates. His presence raises their talent level. Do the same for your business. Talent and brilliance cast a net that soon all will get caught up in.
- Look on each member of your staff not just as a pair of hands and a job function, but as a team player and a source of ideas. Each team may have its superstars, but everyone has an important job to do. No activity is of little importance, just as no team member is of little importance. The big idea or key insight can come from anyone. So use the talent and brains of your people. It's silly to deny yourself the intellectual capabilities and positive attitudes of all your staff. They are aching to make a commitment; give them that opportunity.
- When people are allowed to make decisions, they become increasingly more productive. Having authority is very important to them, whether they use it or not. They feel a sense of importance, independence, respect, and empowerment. This enhances their efficiency and productivity. It is important to be surrounded by people who can make their own decisions: Business moves forward smoothly, problems can be brought to a quicker resolution, and you don't have to waste your time chasing after employees to see if they have completed what they were supposed to do.
- Act on your people's ideas. Let them experiment and make mistakes—within reason. They'll never grow otherwise, and

you'll be closing down a new idea resource bank. An employee may suggest a dozen ideas that produce a benefit of a few dollars each. The next suggestion might be worth $25,000. Reject the first dozen ideas and you don't get the big one.

- Do not take credit yourself for the success of the business. Give that credit or recognition to your people who actually achieved it—and not only at the Christmas party, but regularly throughout the year. When an owner, manager, or coach receives a Super Bowl or World Series trophy, invariably they humbly—and with good reason—step back and say, "This belongs to the players. They're the ones who went out there, battled, and did it." As General George C. Marshall is reputed to have said, "There's no end to what can be accomplished if you credit others."
- People will resent a situation where hard work and extra effort are not rewarded, but only taken advantage of. Rather than feeling an enfranchised part of the business, they'll just feel exploited. Their attitude will become, "Why bother? Where does it get you, anyway?" So give credit where credit is due.
- Share the profits, and you will inspire your people to think and act like owners. The results will amaze you, and the return will be manyfold. Look at the history of Wal-Mart, where profit sharing and stock purchase plans are available to everyone—including the hourly staff. Many of their employees are now millionaires. Share the wealth, and you create further wealth—for your people's wealth is tied to their output. It keeps them focused on being the best.
- Far too many business managers micromanage their operations, nit-pick, and second-guess their staff. What type of message does this send? It only serves to stifle initiative and, to many staff members, can be perceived as a lack of confidence

in them. The real truth often is that the micromanager lacks confidence, hence has the need to doubt or second-guess others. If you feel that you cannot trust or rely on somebody, you should not hire them in the first place.

- Treat your people the way you like to be treated. And as long as you are going to work hard and strive to be the best, enjoy yourself as you do it. Work time is part of your life, and you and your employees should find the greatest value and rewards in it.

LEADERSHIP

A story is told of how General Dwight D. Eisenhower used to demonstrate the art of leadership with a piece of string. He would put it on the table and pull it, and it followed him as he wished. When he tried to push it, it went nowhere. It is just the same in leading people.

> *Managers manage numbers. Leaders lead people.*
>
> *Managers react and solve problems.*
>
> *Leaders set goals . . . develop new ideas . . . motivate their people.*

For too long, business owners and executives intimidated their people and coerced results out of them. Those days are gone. Probably such businesses are also gone.

If staff does not follow the lead voluntarily—that is, they have to be forced—then leadership is lacking. Leadership is not something that is bestowed by virtue of position; rather, it is something you must strive to provide. Those who rely on rank for power are not true leaders. Leaders lead by example and are good motivators. Commitment to a task cannot be compelled; it must be inspired. People must want to follow of their own choice. Leaders work with their people, helping them to do their best and showing them how they can become more productive and useful. Leadership includes helping your critical players develop a sense of where the business is headed, a vision for the future, and the strategies for getting there, then having them buy into it. It also includes creating the environment to enable all this to happen.

The day of the boss as aristocrat-autocrat is over, where edicts were handed down in a kind of corporate despotism. Today, decisions are more collaborative, and the effective contemporary leader is more a facilitator or cheerleader. Today's leader is similar to a movie producer: a leader who brings together the people and conditions for the creativity and optimal outcome to happen. Rather than having absolute control, we're talking about guidance.

Excellent leaders like Sam Walton put their greatest effort into displaying to staff that their work is important and very much appreciated. He actively sought ideas from subordinates on how to improve the business, and would get upset with those who failed to give him bad news. He constantly wanted to improve.

EFFECTIVE LEADERS

Successful businesses are driven by effective leaders. Effective leaders:

- Have a passion for their work, a "fire in the belly." Knowing that having a fire themselves is not sufficient, they transmit it to their people, whom they energize and excite. Effective leaders lead people to action with the power of their convictions and the worthiness of the endeavor.
- Have a vision of where they want to go, and set goals and priorities for their business that are clearly communicated to all.
- Are demanding. They challenge their people to do better.
- Create an atmosphere conducive to bringing out the best in others. They make their people feel that they "belong," which is a very human need and can be a valuable business asset.

- Work with their people and understand the business at all critical levels.
- Continually look for ways to improve the work processes.
- Pay generously so that all feel that they share in the results. Bonuses and profit sharing are important motivators. (Beware, though, of staff coming to expect them as a routine part of their compensation. Additional compensation should be linked to performance and contributions to the company. Bonuses or additional compensation should not be geared solely to financial measures. Revenue growth and profits should be just part of the bonus. The remainder should be tied to customer satisfaction ratings.)
- Drive their business to be the most successful and profitable.

Pursuing these goals enables a leader to be consistent. Effective leadership requires being consistent, not necessarily ingenious. Consistency is of utmost importance. Only when leaders' actions are consistent with the goals established for the business and staff, can they earn the trust of those charged with the responsibility of working toward those goals. Without a motivated and dedicated staff, no leader can be effective.

Effective leaders do not go back on their word or change the rules arbitrarily. When they tell their staff that they will support them in a difficult task, that's exactly what they do. If the leader conveniently forgets the pledge of support, then credibility is lost, probably never to be regained. This happens more frequently than you might think when problems occur with supposed or "titular" leaders. Leaders do not blame others. They accept responsibility themselves. After all, they're in charge. As President Harry S. Truman said, "The buck stops here." A leader must retain credibility at all times, for only in this way will subordinates follow and function with determination and intelligence toward achieving the company's goals.

The ultimate task of an effective leader is to encourage and bring out the best in everyone's work. Staffs look to the leader to set the tone in style and in how things are done, and for approval and positive reinforcement for a job well done. It is not enough to tell people how to do things. You have to lead by example. You don't want to be perceived as a person who says, "Do as I say, not as I do." That doesn't work in parenting; it doesn't work in role modeling as a business leader, either.

As a leader, you need to create a productive, healthy, nurturing, and fulfilling environment for your people. They should enjoy their work because they are being innovative and productive, and because others are supporting and helping them. An effective leader completes the task in a manner that gives the people a feeling of accomplishment and leaves them willing to follow again. With an effective leader, all bask in the glow of accomplishment—and its rewards.

Effective leaders are also excellent motivators. They do so by making the people around them feel important. They show their people that they trust and respect them. Employees treated and regarded in this manner will do all in their power to reciprocate these gestures.

Effective leaders are good listeners and follow up the good listening by asking the opinions of their people. They genuinely honor and care about their people. This point is crucial, for a phony is all too obvious.

Leaders also have a unique sense for the power of enthusiasm. They know that enthusiasm enables them to influence and motivate others. Enthusiasm is an attribute often overlooked in the hiring process, yet it fills one of the three essential qualities of the ACE test described earlier. Without enthusiasm it is difficult to achieve success in any aspect of life, whether personal or business. Surrounding yourself with enthusiastic people can help develop an infectious environment, leading to ever-increasing levels of success.

SUMMARY

To close, leadership is sometimes nothing more than just stepping back, cutting some slack, and letting your best and brightest take the field to "do their thing." Save yourself for the big decisions. Delegate. Today's leaders are no longer lonely at the top. Leadership is very participatory.

2 Every Dollar of Expense Is One Less Dollar of Profit

Expenditure rises to meet income.

—C. Northcote Parkinson

All too often, a business tries to squeeze more out of revenue in the form of price increases rather than by eliminating unnecessary expense. As price levels are usually maximized, expense reduction therefore represents the best—and perhaps the only—opportunity to increase profitability.

Failure to control total overhead to a level that can be supported by sales and resulting gross margins is asking for trouble. The marketplace will not, essentially, "subsidize" more overhead than a business's gross margin will support. The marketplace won't stand for it and won't pay for it. So what are you going to do? What you *have* to do: Get rid of the fat.

Overhead expense is often viewed as an "immovable object" that needs to be covered by a sufficient volume of sales. This form of upside-down logic is what gets businesses into trouble. Control your expenses and you'll control your bottom line. Cost reduction costs virtually nothing. A dollar saved is a dollar added to the bottom line.

It happens that, when squeezed for profit, many businesses will instinctively respond by raising prices. Raising prices frequently just lowers the customer base, which reduces market share. When too many businesses in the same industry raise prices, the result is usually a smaller market as consumers make do with less.

When price increases do not achieve the desired bottom-line effect, some companies addictively just raise prices again. But trying to squeeze out more profits with higher prices just squeezes out even more customers. You only need look at the airline industry as an example. When airlines raise prices, discretionary travelers stay home or bite the bullet and set off for adventures in traveling with the kids on a car trip. When airlines such as Southwest offer reduced fares they expand the size of their market significantly, as a larger segment of the population can afford to take to the skies. With enhanced volume, price reductions—not price increases—are the way to improved profits.

Although price increases are a normal part of business, they can also be an abuse that turns customers away. A desired bottom-line solution can be achieved not by raising prices, but by controlling overhead. High overhead will bury you faster than anything else, so keep your operations lean and efficient.

Warren Avis, in his book *Take a Chance to Be First* (Collier Macmillan, 1986), writes:

> *One of the biggest mistakes most entrepreneurs make is that they fail to keep their expenses under control . . . But at some point, you've got to stand back and put your house in order. That means doing a thorough, systematic, scientific analysis of the costs and expenses and management capabilities in your company.*
>
> *Obviously, it's not possible to lay down the one and only one formula for expenses that will apply perfectly to every business venture . . . But if you'll try to do a better job of controlling your expenses, you'll be taking a giant step toward maximizing your profits.*

Businesses often get fat and happy during periods of prosperity, "loading up" on overhead by converting variable costs—those that fluctuate with business volume—into fixed costs. A large and increasing sales volume often creates the illusion of prosperity, yet all the while expenses are eating up the profit. Staff are added, and often unnecessary expenditures for travel, organization dues, office space, perks, and so on are incurred. These become part of the existing cost structure. Once they have taken root, they create a nightmarish bramble that can take some major excavating to get rid of. The best solution is to not create the problem in the first place.

Increase your profits by reducing expenses. Price increases represent a well that can run dry—a well you can fall into—and soon you're in desperate need of being saved or perhaps are never being heard from again. When you cannot increase your selling prices any further, you've got to lower your costs.

Too many businesses price on a cost-plus basis—that is, cost plus profit equals price. They consider all costs immovable and set their prices accordingly. Satisfied with their profits, they neglect efficiency and head for trouble like lemmings for the sea. Over time, these companies lose market share to their more efficient competitors that have learned to control their expenses. Businesses need to change their thinking to "price minus cost equals profit."

You need to start by asking the question, "If I do away with this expense [or abolish this position], will we lose revenue?" If not, why do you need that expense?

The burden of proof must be switched toward justifying the expenditure and away from justifying its removal. The mind-set or *culture* of the business must be turned around. Instead of the pressure to add costs, the pressure must be to justify what you are currently spending. If you cut costs too much, you can always put it back. But if you spend too much, that money is lost forever.

Lower costs lead to lower prices. Lower prices lead to greater volume, which leads to even lower costs, which in turn lead to still lower prices—thereby perpetuating the cycle. Wal-Mart's overhead expense to sales ratio was nearly 30% less than KMart and 40% less than Sears. How important do you think this has been to its success? Sam Walton was nearly obsessed with reducing expenditures, believing—rightly so—that price would be the most important factor in growing his business. He invested millions of dollars in companywide computer systems and in distribution centers for his stores.

SACRED COWS

Webster's dictionary defines a *sacred cow* as "a person or thing immune from criticism." Every business has its sacred cows, sometimes known as "it's always been that way." Nobody questions them, because they're comfortable or they don't want to rock the boat. Much of the waste and many of the problems in business, and in government, exist because they have been perpetuated through historical precedent. What was a good idea once is not necessarily a good idea now.

Businesses invest a great deal of effort, time, and money to feed their sacred cows. To be effective in your efforts at cost control—and to display to your staff that you are serious in the endeavor—no position, procedure, system, policy, habit, division, or line of business should go unquestioned. Everything must be reviewed, irrespective of its history. "It's always been that way" is not sufficient justification to leave anything unquestioned. No cost is sacred. Here's what to do:

- Isolate any procedures, systems, policies, or habits that are outdated and streamline them.
- Identify the unproductive or busy work that management and staff engage in. Are those long, boring morning meetings productive? Do so many people have to attend? How about capping the meeting at 30 minutes? Are all those memos necessary, or are they just ego trips for the writers?

- Take a number of different transactions and trace them step by step through the entire process from their initiation to their culmination with the payment by the customer. Seek to uncomplicate things. Be on the lookout for:
  —Overlap or duplication of effort.
  —Unnecessary slowdowns as the transaction moves through the system.
  —Unnecessary steps in the process.
  —Unnecessary paperwork.
  —More efficient approaches to completing the various steps.

To overcome employee resistance to slaughtering sacred cows, emphasize to them the importance of change and how it is in their own self-interest as well as that of their company. For without a profitable company, you're out of business and they're out of a job.

EXCESSIVE (NONPRODUCTIVE) STAFF

Staffs tend to fatten up rather than slim down. A common business solution to a problem is to "hire somebody." However, throwing bodies at a problem does not solve anything. Frequently it makes things worse. When this is the solution to every problem, it does not take too long before the payroll is bloated. Overstaffing often leads to a lazy environment where nothing gets done. You do not need a body for every title. Staff can assume a number of titles or roles.

Beware of academically minded individuals on your staff. They like to do everything "by the book." They add unnecessary departments, produce unnecessary reports, add layers of fat, hire people into nonproductive positions, and have six people doing the job of one.

Also be aware of those who are in over their head, for they often surround themselves with extra staff for protection and can be jealous of and limit your most promising recruits.

Watch out for empire builders—they hire assistants, deputies, assistants to the deputies, and secretaries for everybody. Pretty soon, everyone is drowning in memos, reports, meetings, and so on—having totally lost focus of what their role is supposed to be.

Take a step back and compare your business volume today with a point in the past when your staffing levels were leaner. Then, compare the number of staff engaged today in the various functions with those engaged in the past. You may be surprised with what you find.

Larger-than-necessary staffs spend too much time interacting with each other, rather than being productive.

In many businesses, some 40% of the jobs are bureaucratic and do not make any direct revenue contribution to the company. The usefulness or need for all non–revenue-producing individuals should be examined closely. Evaluate each position as it relates to producing a quality product, satisfying customers, and/or assisting management to make decisions. Eliminate the positions, especially those in middle and upper management, that add to the bureaucracy and make no truly worthwhile contribution. There should be no more than two levels of staff between the CEO and the lowest level staff person, or four levels in all. Flatten your organization chart.

Every business has two types of staff: those who do the productive work and bring in the revenue, and those who "manage." The latter type should be the focus of much of your attention.

Reducing your staffing forces those remaining to eliminate the inefficient and unnecessary work efforts in the system. It forces them to prioritize and to focus on the truly important work efforts that need to be undertaken. The "busy work" will be eliminated.

Downsizing is not just for large businesses. Small and midsize businesses can realize significant profit enhancements through working smarter. Entrepreneurs and business executives are often so focused on sales and customer service as a means of growing profits that they overlook some of the more obvious opportunities right under their nose for multiplying profits. A business with a 5% net profit margin and 20% of revenue expended on administrative staff can double its profits to 10% with a 25% cutback in administrative staff salaries. This is not as far-fetched as you may initially think. I have achieved these results for clients. In every business there are staff who do not pull their full weight or are unnecessary and do not contribute to the profitability of the enterprise. These people are being targeted here.

If it cannot be established that the output of each individual is vital to producing the company's product, enhancing quality, servicing customers, or developing new markets, consideration should be given to eliminating that position.

Staff should be evaluated by the quality of the results they produce, rather than by how many hours they work. There is often little correlation between hours worked and results achieved. Beware of individuals or departments who continually put in a great deal of overtime. Occasional overtime is necessary to compensate for surges in business or busy periods. But continuous overtime, more often than not, identifies a lack of organization on the part of the individual or department management.

SALES COMMISSIONS

Many smaller businesses are dissatisfied with their sales compensation plans, but are wary of venturing into the unknown to change them. They feel that their pay plans fail to motivate their staffs to make an extra effort, and are concerned that they are overcompensating poor performers. But still, they take no action.

Many businesses outgrow their compensation plans. As young, single-product enterprises, they offered the same commission rate on all sales. However, when they add to their product lines, this approach encourages sales staff to coast on commissions from the established lines and customers rather than promote the new products.

Businesses should gear commissions to the effort involved in making the sale. They should have graduated commission rates based on the degree of difficulty in making the sale and the profitability yielded. Switch your commission system from a sales-based to a profit margin–based approach. The results should surprise you as the emphasis shifts to selling the more profitable products.

Sales staff should not be allowed to coast along as mere order takers. Certainly it is important to keep the present customer base satisfied; however, this should not be the sole purpose of the salespeople's existence. They should be constantly seeking new sources of business, and for that they should be rewarded with a higher commission rate. A diminishing rate can be paid on subsequent orders. In this way, they will be constantly motivated to keep producing new sales.

HOW TO MANAGE EXPENSES

Expense reduction is similar to dieting: The fat always tries to return and stays away only with constant vigilance and maintenance of healthy habits. Managing expenses must be an ongoing process during both good times and bad. Embarking on a crash diet every time business turns sour is too reactive and can lead to desperation-driven decisions. Instead, constant vigilance is necessary to take care of small problems before they become big problems. The fundamental problem or behavior that caused the excess costs in the first place needs to be identified and eliminated.

Increasing profits through expense reduction must be based on an organized, planned program where there are no absolute rules. Judgment must be used in assessing each item of expenditure, as you don't want to cut out muscle with the fat. An accounting system providing the relevant amount of detail is necessary to ascertain and analyze the costs. Such records will provide the figures to prepare a profit and loss statement (preferably monthly), a budget, break-even calculations, and evaluations of your operating ratios compared with the norms for your industry.

Simply slashing expenses across the board is like blowing fish out of the water: You get your fish—but there is damage, inefficiency, and overkill. Management must understand the nature of each expense item and how each interrelates with sales, inventory, cost of goods sold, gross profits, overhead expense, and operating profit.

Expense reduction does not only mean eliminating certain expenses. You can achieve greater profit through more efficient use of the expense dollar. Sometimes you cannot cut an expense item, but you can get more from it and thus increase your profit. For example, if you increase sales and keep the dollar amount of an expense the same, you have decreased that expense as a percentage of sales. When you decrease your cost percentage, you increase your profit percentage. In other words, you have improved the productivity of your expenses.

An understanding of the worth of each expense item comes from experience and an analysis of the records. This analysis provides data that can help you set realistic cost and profit goals.

ORGANIZATIONAL ANALYSIS

The intent of organizational analysis is to ascertain how businesses can be reorganized and streamlined to increase effectiveness and productivity and possibly to reduce cost. Everyone should get a hard look. No one should be exempt. This is not an impossible task. After all, we are not dealing with a huge multinational corporation. The information needed is a current organization chart, with the salaries noted thereon.

There are a number of rules to follow when conducting such an analysis:

- There should not be more than four staff levels in the company. The CEO occupies the first level, and three more levels follow. Minimizing the number of layers is important in order to involve all staff in the decision-making process. It also prevents an unnecessary layer of fat from accumulating.

- The CEO and those in senior management should usually have from seven to 10 individuals reporting to them. Any less that this, and you may have an unnecessary management level or position.
- Managers responsible for the departments that most impact profits should report to the CEO; for example, the head of purchasing in a manufacturing organization is often responsible for up to 50% of the expense incurred but often reports to a much lower level.

RATIO ANALYSIS

It is important to be systematic and detailed as you develop the expense picture for your company. You should have five years of relevant detail available to work with, preferably on a computerized spreadsheet. Your accounting department should provide the following data in totals for each of the five years:

- Sales
- Materials
- Labor
- Overhead costs
- Gross margin
- Selling costs
- General and administrative (G&A) expense
- Operating profit
- Interest expense
- Other income/expense
- Before-tax income

The example here is for a manufacturing firm. The same approach can be used for a service business through use of the appropriate detail for direct expenses.

Comparing the data for the five years presents the following interesting comparison:

Company Data
($ in thousands)

	Sales	Materials		Labor		Plant		Profit margin	
	$	$	%	$	%	$	%	$	%
Year 1	32000	12800	40.0	4800	15.0	1600	5.0	12800	40.0
Year 2	34000	13260	39.0	4930	14.5	1632	4.8	14178	41.7
Year 3	40000	16320	40.8	6040	15.1	1880	4.7	15760	39.4
Year 4	45000	17055	37.9	7830	17.4	2745	6.1	17370	38.6
Year 5	50000	19250	38.5	8450	16.9	2900	5.8	19400	38.8
Industry average			38.2%		15.0%		4.5%		42.3%

Expenses
($ in thousands)

	Selling		G&A		Interest		Operating profit	
	$	%	$	%	$	%	$	%
Year 1	3520	11.0	5760	18.0	960	3.0	2560	8.0
Year 2	4114	12.1	6358	18.7	884	2.6	2822	8.3
Year 3	5440	13.6	7400	18.5	1240	3.1	1680	4.2
Year 4	5715	12.7	9405	20.9	1485	3.3	765	1.7
Year 5	6950	13.9	11100	22.2	1800	3.6	<450>	<0.9>
Industry average		12.9%		18.5%		1.8%		9.1%

This first step is an overview or macro analysis of the data by category, as we seek to understand what has happened with this business. Looking at the best-case scenario derived from taking the best ratios over the five years, one can see that the business could be immensely profitable with a pretax profit margin of 11.3%. Instead, it is showing a loss on revenues of $50 million.

This exercise is important for every business to conduct at least annually. Rather than simply relying upon the current financial data to gain a perspective of the business, you need a frame of reference—some data to compare your results against. Otherwise you can be operating in a vacuum. Five years of data can provide a reasonable perspective, although seven or 10 years' worth would be even better.

What do we learn from our example?

1. Sales growth has been excellent, growing by 56% over five years.
2. The gross profit peaked at 41.7% in year 2, and we are now at 38.8%. The average for the five years was 39.7%.
3. Material cost at 38.5% in the latest year contrasts well with the average of 39.2% for the five years. This is helping the gross profit percentage.
4. Labor cost has risen appreciably in the last two years, although it has fallen somewhat in the latest year. This area needs to be looked at. If there was not a large wage increase granted in year 4, overstaffing or lack of productivity must have given rise to the present situation.
5. Plant costs have also risen in the last two years. This needs to be investigated further.
6. Selling costs and G&A expense is where the majority of the problem is. Selling expense is at 13.9%. The average for the previous four years was 12.3%. G&A at 22.2% is 3.2% higher than the average of the previous four years.

The increase in selling cost could be partly attributable to the tremendous growth in sales over the five years. However, unless the current data in year 6 is showing a significant increase in sales over the previous year, a comprehensive study starting with an organizational analysis needs to be undertaken.

The increase in G&A expense is symptomatic of a company lulled into a false sense of complacency by its tremendous sales growth. A large increase in sales volume often creates the illusion of prosperity while, in reality, expenses are eating up the profit. We will undertake a microanalysis of this area to spot what improvements can be made.

7. Interest expense is rising also; however, this is probably due to the loss-making situation in which the business finds itself. Improve the bottom line, and you will reduce your indebtedness and interest expense.

Microanalysis of G&A Costs
(% of sales dollar)

	Year 1	Year 2	Year 3	Year 4	Year 5
Officers' salaries	2.0	1.9	1.9	2.5	3.0
Management salaries	5.6	5.8	5.7	6.1	6.6
Office salaries	4.0	4.3	4.3	4.4	4.5
Payroll taxes	1.2	1.2	1.2	1.2	1.2
Employee benefits	2.5	2.6	2.6	2.6	2.5
Insurance	1.0	1.0	1.0	1.0	0.9
Dues	—	—	—	0.2	0.3
Leased autos	—	—	—	0.2	0.3
Telephone	0.25	0.3	0.25	0.3	0.2
Office supplies	0.25	0.25	0.3	0.3	0.2
Legal fees	0.1	0.1	0.1	0.1	0.2

Accounting fees	0.1	0.1	0.1	0.1	0.15
Consultants' fees	—	—	—	0.1	0.2
Rent	0.5	0.5	0.5	1.0	0.9
Postage	0.05	0.05	0.05	0.05	0.05
Data processing	0.2	0.15	0.1	0.15	0.15
Utilities	0.1	0.15	0.1	0.15	0.15
Travel	0.1	0.1	0.1	0.15	0.3
Entertainment	0.05	0.2	0.2	0.3	0.4
Total	18.0	18.7	18.5	20.9	22.2

In year 5,

$$1.0\% = \$500{,}000$$
$$0.1\% = \$50{,}000$$

One need not be a rocket scientist to see what has happened here—the ownership and the management got "fat and happy." For example,

- Officers' salaries at 3% comes to $1,500,000 annually. Spouses, children, and grandchildren are probably on the payroll.
- Management and office salaries have grown much faster than the business's rate of growth.
- Some perks for those in high places have crept into the picture. Club dues are $150,000, and so is leased auto expense and travel expense. Entertainment is now running at $200,000. As phenomenal as these figures are, they are not as outrageous as what I have seen in some businesses.
- Swankier offices were obviously taken on in year 4.

- Legal, accounting, and consulting fees are starting to grow because somebody in the company is starting to panic and looking for advice. These fees will probably grow much higher in the subsequent year when management realizes that this business needs some good advice to help get its act together.

What advice would you give to this business? Take time to ponder this question before going on.

My solution? They need to go back to what made them successful in the first place. The business is obviously successful; sales are going at a great rate and profit margins are pretty constant, other than a problem with direct labor and plant cost. So they are doing something right. They just need to stop spending money foolishly. The officers need to set the example and take a sizeable pay cut, then eliminate any family ghost payrollers. Management and office salaries have also become bloated with the prosperity, and they need to be trimmed.

Salary cutbacks will provide a ripple benefit to payroll taxes, employee benefits, and insurance as they will fall proportionately.

The expense for club dues, leased autos, travel, and entertainment should be cut back to its year 1 level.

The solutions to turning a business around are often quite straightforward. Just use common sense—although at times common sense is not too common! You only have a problem when you don't recognize that you have a problem. Recognition and acceptance is more than half the battle.

QUALITY

Institute a quality program. Many businesses with the highest quality usually have the lowest costs and generally experience an overall improvement in performance ranging from increased market share to better employee relations, greater customer satisfaction, higher productivity, and continued profitability.

Total quality management (TQM) is a beneficial program for businesses both large and small and is not only for companies engaged in the manufacture or selling of "thing"-type products; service companies of any size can also benefit from using a TQM approach.

Historically, businesses regarded quality improvement as not cost-effective. "It'll cost us time and money," the thinking went. "So we lose a few customers. We'll more than make up for it with extra volume." This thinking was back to front. Quality improvement can actually save time and money—and a customer base. It's worth a great deal to any business not having to:

- Follow up on customer complaints.
- Repack and restock customer returns.
- Increase advertising and sales promotion outlays to recover lost market share as a result of either poor quality or a level of quality that can't compete.
- Collect from dissatisfied customers who feel that they were not provided quality products/services in the first place.
- Engage in a costly crisis management public relations campaign to assure a nervous marketplace that you are a quality operation.
- Handle labor disagreements with employees who feel victimized or mistreated. (TQM also helps to keep employee morale high.)
- Be embroiled in possible litigation or bad press from substandard products or services.

All too often, business considered quantity as important as—or even more important than—quality. That's an attitude left over from the 1950s, where a post–World War II marketplace voraciously absorbed whatever was offered, and mass production in and of itself meant lower costs. Everybody knows where that type of thinking got the American automobile industry. The fact is that without quality, quantity is irrelevant.

Quality pays. Businesses with the highest quality often have the lowest costs. Businesses can reduce their costs by improving quality. Many have found that they were carrying large, hidden costs due to producing inferior products and services. TQM, by improving the quality of products and services, reduces the costs associated with inferior quality. High-quality businesses can usually charge premium prices. Improved quality builds market share, which in turn translates into increased profitability. This all can be accomplished through an effective TQM program.

PURCHASING

The importance of purchasing depends on the percentage of your total expenditures that materials represents. For an advertising agency it would be close to zero, therefore no emphasis would be required. For manufacturing and retail outlets, purchasing usually represents the greatest source of expenditures. Purchasing correctly therefore represents the best opportunity to reduce expenditures. For example, a 10% reduction in material costs in a business where materials represent 50% of the sales dollar would translate into a 5% addition to operating profit. A business with a 5% bottom line will have doubled its profits! Since materials can represent such a large chunk of all expenditures, does it not stand to reason that this area can produce the greatest impact in reducing expenditures? Therefore, does it not make sense that the purchasing department get the recognition it deserves?

The head of purchasing should be at the same level as other department heads. Don't relegate him or her to a management level two flights down. If you do, you're saying that purchasing only involves order placing and therefore is not important. The purchasing department must be regarded as an instrumental part of any cost-cutting program. The cost of materials can be reduced with existing personnel.

How to Do It

Establish an A-B-C classification system to prioritize all materials and parts purchased.

An A classification pertains to the most expensive items, items that are usually very important to the business operation. They may make up some 75% of the cost of the materials, but represent perhaps up to 10% in volume. These are the items where the majority of your money is going, and therefore they require the greatest emphasis. Cost reduction should concentrate mainly on these items.

The B-type materials are those that are less expensive than the A types and represent some 20% of your purchases.

The C types are the most inexpensive, the standard parts that are used all the time. They usually represent about 5% of total inventory.

Now that we have identified those parts where your focus should be concentrated, here are some suggestions on how to go about lowering your cost:

- Establish a goal for the purchasing department to meet, in terms of materials cost reduction, whether it be 5%, 8%, or 10% over 12 months. They must have something to shoot for. Provide assistance and encouragement to them as they strategize to meet the goal. Don't just dump the task on them and walk away. Now for the important part: The first rule of negotiating is to limit the negotiator's authority. Empower them to accept concessions, but not to give them.
- Also, keep in mind that salespeople are usually awful negotiators. They are so keen to make the sale that they will drop the price. First, however, they must be convinced that the sale depends on their dropping the price.
- Competition is obviously the key. Staying with the supplier because "it's worked well in the past" or because "that's what we have always done" does not mean that the supplier has necessarily remained competitive. When qualified vendors,

with the right quality product, offer a lower bid on an item, they should be awarded all or a portion of the business. Do not turn around and ask your present supplier to match their prices. Favoritism to one supplier will discourage others from continuing to offer low bids.

- Declare a price freeze. Some suppliers will ignore your announcement, but many will go along with it.
- Or, declare that every price increase will automatically trigger a competitive bidding situation. That will scare many increases away.
- Ascertain what your competitors are paying. Knowledge is power.
- An open door policy must be a priority. Salespeople are not a nuisance. They can help you lower your costs! They must know that the door to the purchasing department is always open to them. Such a policy makes your business accessible to new and innovative ideas. New techniques are created every day.
- Avoid locking yourself into one supplier—not only for competitive purposes, but to ensure that you have an alternative were that supplier to find itself in difficulty due to a strike or some such event. You must ensure a steady, thrifty, and uninterrupted flow of materials, and you can achieve this with multiple sources.
- To enhance cash flow, use vendor stocking. Have them maintain their inventory on your premises and charge for it as drawn upon for use.
- The purchasing department should not necessarily accept the final quoted price. Costs can always be reduced further, and the purchasers must assume that there is fat in every number. This is where their buyer's experience and expertise can be useful. Explore various possibilities with the vendors. Is there a cheaper way to deliver the product? Can some of the packing

be eliminated? Would purchasing in larger quantities reduce the cost? Would it save to use your own vehicles to pick it up? Can you purchase from a vendor in the off-season where they may be willing to charge you on an incremental basis to cover the labor and direct costs, just to keep their plant operating? Can you work with your suppliers to make them more efficient? Can you standardize some items, and use only a single supplier?

- Seek ideas from your suppliers. Since they usually deal with a wide range of businesses, they can often make suggestions about new products or design improvements. It never hurts to ask.
- If it has not already been done, it should be made quite clear to all concerned that gifts and gratuities from vendors are not acceptable. A letter to this effect should go out to all suppliers annually.

It is unlikely that any area in your business provides a greater opportunity to save on costs than purchasing. Frequently, however, it is most often overlooked.

YOUR EXPENSES

In reviewing your expense detail, consider such questions as:

- How much does each item contribute to profits? This is a very difficult question to quantify, and all must give it serious thought. All expenses must contribute and translate into increased revenue, improved quality, customer satisfaction, and, ultimately, profits. If an expense item cannot justify its existence, why keep it around?
- Are any of these expenses unusually high?
- Are all of these expenses necessary for conducting business—for example, association dues, image advertising, travel, entertainment, legal fees, space, company cars, cellular telephones?
- How do our expenses by type compare with the norms for our industry?

- Is the lowest possible price being paid for each item and service—for example, by obtaining competitive bids, and revising these costs regularly?

Other specific cost reduction ideas to consider include the following:

- Eliminate low-margin or low-volume products, providing that you also eliminate the costs associated with them. Do not eliminate the revenue and leave the cost.
- Dispose of, or close down, unprofitable divisions, subsidiaries, or plants.
- Is there excessive discounting?
- Provide incentives to encourage cost reduction ideas from the staff.
- Conduct employee skill improvement programs to improve productivity.
- Improve sales forecasting procedures to provide for more efficient production planning and reduced inventory levels.
- Can the sales effort be reorganized—by territory or function—to enhance sales?
- Review all promotional costs to determine whether they sufficiently benefit the business.
- Review all of the staff positions in the company and ask the following questions:

  —What does the position really do?

  —Do we actually need this position?

  —Can the position be combined with that of another?
- The CEO should sign or approve all non-payroll checks to track where the cash is going. Doing so can deter frivolous spending and often reveal wasteful practices.

- Do you hire consultants to make decisions that should be made internally or to cover somebody's tail should something go wrong?
- Request, of all employees, suggestions on how to:

  —Accelerate the work flow.

  —Solve persistent problems.

  —Eliminate wasteful procedures.

  —Improve operations.
- Reward employees through the use of a bonus system for improving their own productivity.
- Do not allow an overqualified person, at a much higher salary, to fill a less demanding position.
- Is their excess supervision? Not all supervisors or managers are necessary. They should have at least seven to 10 people reporting to them, if not more.
- On preparing the annual budget/financial plan:

  —Reexamine all spending, rather than just adding to the prior year's figure.

  —Consider whether last year's spending was as effective as possible.

  —Are there areas where spending could be reduced?
- Automate. Machines don't go on strike, call in sick, or sue you. They are an excellent investment in producing long-term productivity gains.
- The managers of many businesses all too often call their lawyers every time they think they have a problem. This can be a very expensive solution. Lawyers sell time, and usually at very high rates.
- Does your cost accounting system identify unprofitable products or divisions?

- Can changes be made to reduce distribution cost—for example, by using trucks, aircraft, or rail, or by relocating distribution centers?
- Flowchart the work flow to identify duplicative and redundant steps.
- When staff cuts are necessary, don't cut across the board. Target those with the poorest attitudes and work output.
- Cross-train staff for maximum efficiency and employee development.
- Consider whether new or upgraded software could improve productivity or reduce the number of personnel.
- Be aware of all new expenditures. If the business was operating without them previously, are they really necessary now? What do they contribute?
- Approve all purchases above a certain dollar amount and review a random sample of all other purchases. Pay attention to small details. Ensure that all invoices, purchase orders, and receiving reports are attached to check requests. Review the invoices to ascertain what is being purchased, the quantity, and the unit price.
- Do you always obtain competing bids?
- Are you alert to volume discounts?
- Do you search for new suppliers with lower costs?
- Do you accept price increases as inevitable?
- Is there excess plant or office capacity? Most businesses occupy twice as much space as they really need.
- Are labor costs tracked and compared with the industry norm?
- Is overtime a problem?
- Do you identify and correct the causes of production delays?
- Are materials or energy being wasted?

Reducing expenses can be far more profitable than increasing sales. If your company makes a 10% profit after all costs are covered, $1000 in sales minus $900 in costs produces a profit of $100. A 10% increase in sales will increase profit by $10. A 10% reduction in cost saves $90, or nine times as much. Thus, a reduction in cost of 1.1% will produce as much profit as a 10% increase in sales. Think about it.

Many successful managers make it an overriding priority to find and control their costs. You should too. Being tied up in day-to-day affairs and not having the time is no excuse. The fact is that there is probably no more productive or profitable way in which you can spend your time.

Most executives are of the belief that sales growth is their first priority. Sales are terribly important to a business; however, as we have seen, cost reduction can have a much greater impact on the bottom line. Executives would prefer to build up the sales volume to a sufficient level to cover the overhead rather than face the task of cutting out the fat and laying people off. It is this logic that causes the problem in the first place.

Cost reduction and control must become a way of life for all businesses. The example must come from the top, otherwise lower-level staff will not pursue the task with the diligence that it deserves. It should involve all employees, particularly those closest to the action. They must be provided with the authority, training, and skills necessary to make a worthwhile contribution to the cost control efforts.

Resistance to change will be your greatest obstacle. People are afraid of change; they don't like rocking the boat. But stick with it. Small steps lead to big steps. Big steps multiply profits.

3 Cash Flow Is the Name of the Game

A business lives or dies on cash flow. Sales are great and profits are wonderful, but cash flow governs whether or not you succeed.

Every business—from a 25¢ lemonade stand to a $25 billion corporation—functions on cash. Cash is the energy source that pulsates through a company and keeps the business running, surviving, and thriving. Without a healthy cash flow circulating through it, ailments and weakness will occur that can lead to the diminishment and/or death of the business.

Recognizing that your suppliers and payroll are paid from cash, not profits, is important. You cannot make the payroll with receivables or inventory. Profits are nice, but they are only on paper until they are turned into that very special legal tender paper you can take to the bank.

Profits are only realized when a product or service has been rendered and payment received. At that point, profits turn into cash—and then you can pay your bills and accumulate cash reserves. Thus, an adequate capitalization and cash flow are vital to maintaining a successful business. Cash and working capital are what help give you a good night's rest.

The cash flow cycle should be properly understood by owners and managers:

- Cash levels are reduced when goods and services are purchased and paid for.
- The products and/or services are sold, and these sales generate either cash or accounts receivable.
- When the customer pays your billing, the cash balance increases and accounts receivable decreases.

Thus, there is a time lapse between the time a product or service is purchased and cash payment is received for that product or service. The duration of that time lapse is very important because it directly affects your cash flow—and your cash flow is not only a barometer of your financial health, it is primarily how you pay your own bills and payroll and limit your borrowing expenses.

Cash flow forecasting is not just for large firms. The managements of many small and midsize businesses often fail to recognize the benefits of such planning. It can:

- Highlight those periods when raising a bank loan or other form of financing to cover a need may be necessary. Doing this in advance is easier, rather than after the need has arisen.
- Determine the time for repayment of borrowings.
- Pinpoint a period of cash surplus that could be used for the purchase of inventory or equipment.
- Act as an indicator of an ongoing or oncoming cash shortfall, thus anticipating the need for additional capitalization for the business.

The cash flow statement, or forecast, tells a great deal about the present and future health of your business. You must have one.

Owners of many profitable businesses sometimes observe with consternation, "We are doing gang-buster sales, our profits are up, but why is the bank balance so low?" One reason is that profits are not necessarily reflected in a bank balance. Understanding that cash flow and profit are not the same is important. Profit is an accounting concept, whereas cash flow is an operating concept.

- Profit is the difference between sales and expenses.
- Cash flow is the difference between receipts and disbursements.
- Profit is calculated without regard to whether monies have actually been received or disbursed.
- Cash flow considers only money actually entering or leaving the company.

When profits move in one direction, cash often moves in the opposite direction. Having a negative cash flow is frequently possible for a profitable company, as the upcoming example will show.

FAST GROWTH CORPORATION

Let's consider the example of the Fast Growth Corporation. Its vital signs at the beginning of the fiscal year are:

- Cash in the bank of $35,000
- Receivables of $70,000
- Inventory of $80,000
- No payables

Each unit that it purchases costs $8 and sells for $10. All receivables are collected in full the following month. There are no bad debts. The receivables of $70,000 are collected in full in the first month of the new year, raising the cash level to $105,000. All inventory is sold in full the following month.

What a great business! Making 20% profit on sales! 100% of receivables are collected on a timely basis! Inventory turns over in full every month.

Its sales and inventory purchases are as follows:

	Units sold	Units purchased
January	10,000	12,500
February	12,500	15,000
March	15,000	20,000

Now let us look at the profitability of the business during these months:

	January	**February**	**March**
		Profit and Loss	
Opening inventory	$ 80,000	$ 100,000	$ 120,000
Purchases	100,000	120,000	160,000
Closing inventory	<100,000>	<120,000>	<160,000>
Cost of sales	80,000	100,000	120,000
Sales	100,000	125,000	150,000
Profit	20,000	$ 25,000	$ 30,000
Cumulative profit		**$ 45,000**	**$ 75,000**

What a tremendous profit for only three months of business activity! Now let us look at the cash flow side of the business:

	January Cash Flow	**February Cash Flow**	**March Cash Flow**
Opening cash	$ 35,000	$ 5,000	$ <15,000>
Receivables collection	70,000	100,000	125,000
Inventory purchases	<100,000>	<120,000>	<160,000>
Closing cash	$ 5,000	$< 15,000>	$ <50,000>

How could a business that earned a profit of $75,000 in three months go from a positive cash balance of $35,000 to a negative cash balance of $50,000 in the same time period? What happened to bring this situation about? What happened to the profit? Let us explore and consider the business's vital signs (see Figure 3.1). Sales are increasing rapidly every month—no problem there.

The cash balance is moving in the opposite direction of sales (see Figure 3.2). Where has the cash gone? Figures 3.3 and 3.4 will reveal the culprits! Accounts receivable has grown to $150,000, an increase of $80,000. Inventory has also grown appreciably, from $80,000 to $160,000. This represents an increase of $80,000.

A reconciliation of the foregoing is in order for those who might think they have just witnessed a juggling act with numbers.

Balance Sheet as of March 31

Assets		
Accounts receivable		$150,000
Inventory		160,000
		$310,000
Liabilities and equity		
Cash overdrawn		$ 50,000
Opening equity position		
Cash	35,000	
Receivables	70,000	
Inventory	80,000	
	$185,000	
Cumulative profit	75,000	260,000
		$310,000

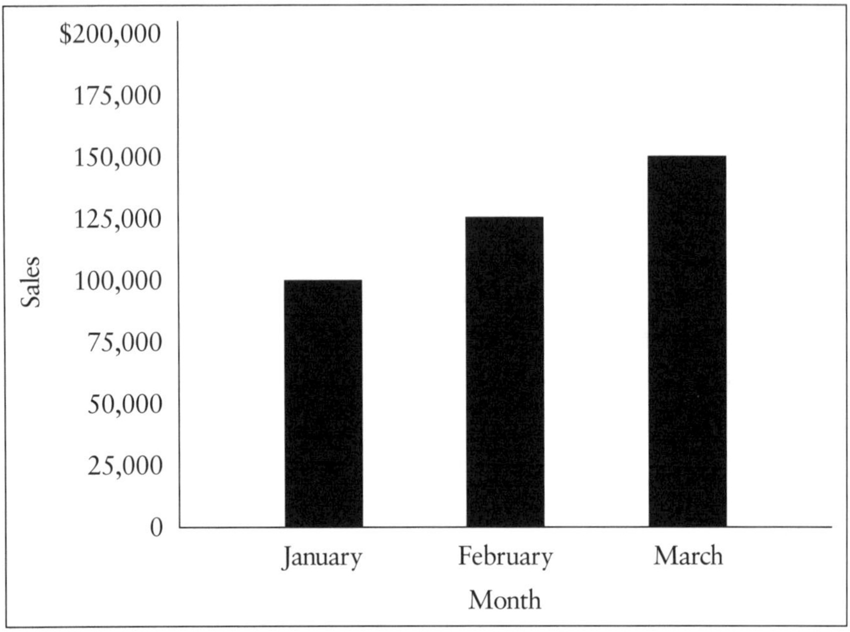

Figure 3.1. Sales growth.

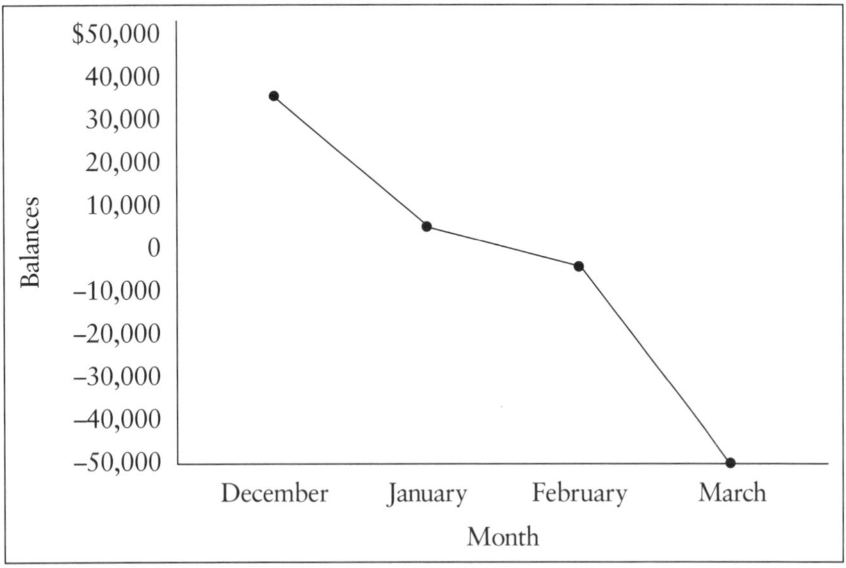

Figure 3.2. Cash balances.

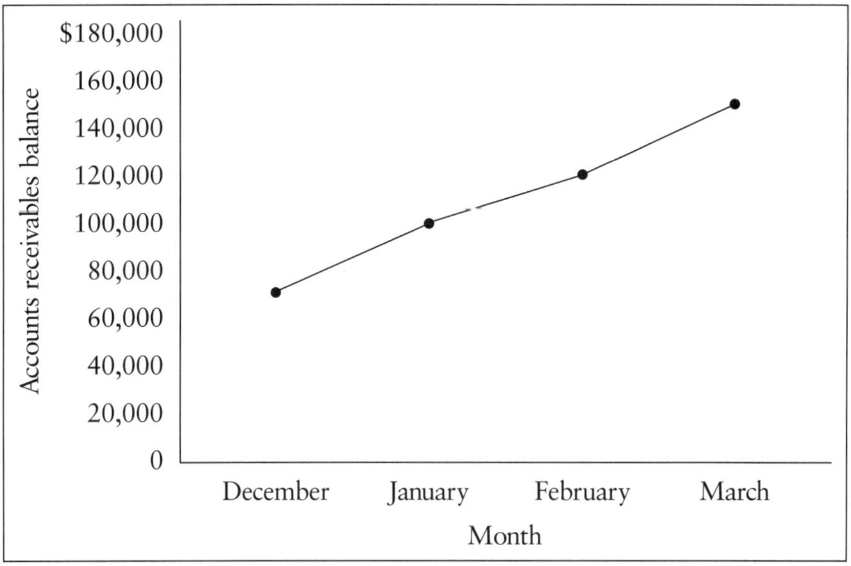

Figure 3.3. Accounts receivable.

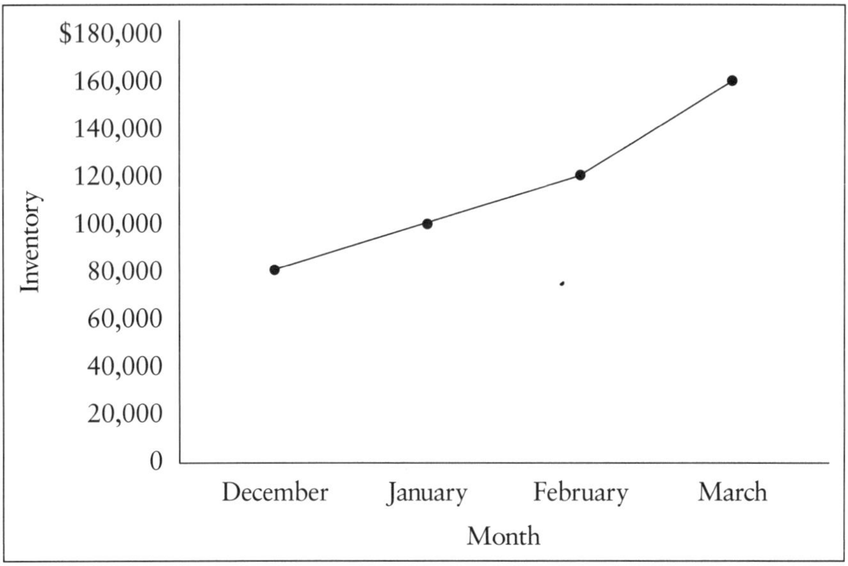

Figure 3.4. Inventory.

While the business has been very profitable, these profits have been swallowed up by the need to finance the rapid growth. The receivables and inventory have to be financed for the business to continue.

Looking down the road, the business obviously cannot continue at its present rate of fast growth. The cash flow is simply not there to finance it. Assuming the absence of any additional financing, what can be done?

Let us examine its profitability and cash flow if the business froze its activity level in April, May, and June to the March inventory level of 20,000 units, or $160,000.

	April
	Profit and Loss
Opening inventory	$ 160,000
Purchases	160,000
Closing inventory	<160,000>
Cost of sales	160,000
Sales	200,000
Profit	$ 40,000

The profit for May and June would be the same as April, as we have frozen activity at that level for the three month period. Now let us review the cash flow position for these three months.

	April Cash Flow
Opening cash	$ <50,000>
Receivables collection	150,000
Inventory purchases	<160,000>
Closing cash	$ <60,000>

The cash position has worsened, but only because the March sales—collected in April—were less than the April inventory purchased. The cash flow situation should start to turn around in May when the unit sales level begins to match the inventory purchased.

	May Cash Flow
Opening cash	$ <60,000>
Receivables collection	200,000
Inventory purchases	<160,000>
Closing cash	$ <20,000>

Since the inventory level has been frozen, the entire month's profit of $40,000 goes to pay down the cash overdraft.

	June Cash Flow
Opening cash	$ <20,000>
Receivables collection	200,000
Inventory purchases	<160,000>
Closing cash	$ 20,000

Finally the business has turned the corner on its cash flow.

The point of this exercise is to emphasize that profit and cash flow do not go hand in hand. As a business grows, it needs the financial resources to fund inventory and receivables. There is a time delay from when you purchase inventory to when you sell it on credit to when you receive the cash. This time lapse requires cash to fund it. Many entrepreneurs and business managers fail to understand that more sales initially mean reduced cash flow, and that reduced cash flow can spell trouble.

The fundamental problem with the business in this example is that the company was overtrading given its financial resources available. This is very common with many businesses today. Either they must obtain additional financing to provide the necessary funds for growth, or they have to temper their growth to the financial resources available.

The inability to manage a business's cash needs is a primary cause for the demise of many profitable enterprises, such as could have occurred in the example. Many businesses that measure success only by their level of profit are shocked when facing unpaid creditors and no cash in the bank. It is common to see them stop paying their withholding taxes, which is not only against the law, but downright stupid—for the government, with its interest and penalties, charges rates similar to those levied by organized crime. It is a nightmare, so do not let it happen.

Figure 3.5 illustrates the trend of cash flow problems for the Fast Growth Corporation. As the figure shows, when the business was on a growth spurt from January through March, its inventory and receivables shot up and its cash balance plummeted. Only when its sales volume was frozen for April, May, and June did the inventory and receivables level off and the cash balance recover.

Many failures occur in businesses with high growth rates. Cash flow problems can drown a successful business in its own paper prosperity. To avoid this, plan for growth. Consider the growth margins, additional overhead required, and payment delay. Had this business prepared cash flow projections, management could have been prepared for these problems. Unfortunately, many small and midsize businesses focus solely on the bottom line, with little thought given to cash flow. As stated earlier, your payroll and suppliers are paid from cash, not profits—although, of course, profits ultimately become cash.

A high-growth business is always paying for tomorrow's big sales growth with yesterday's small receivables collection. Unless such a business is well capitalized and management exercises

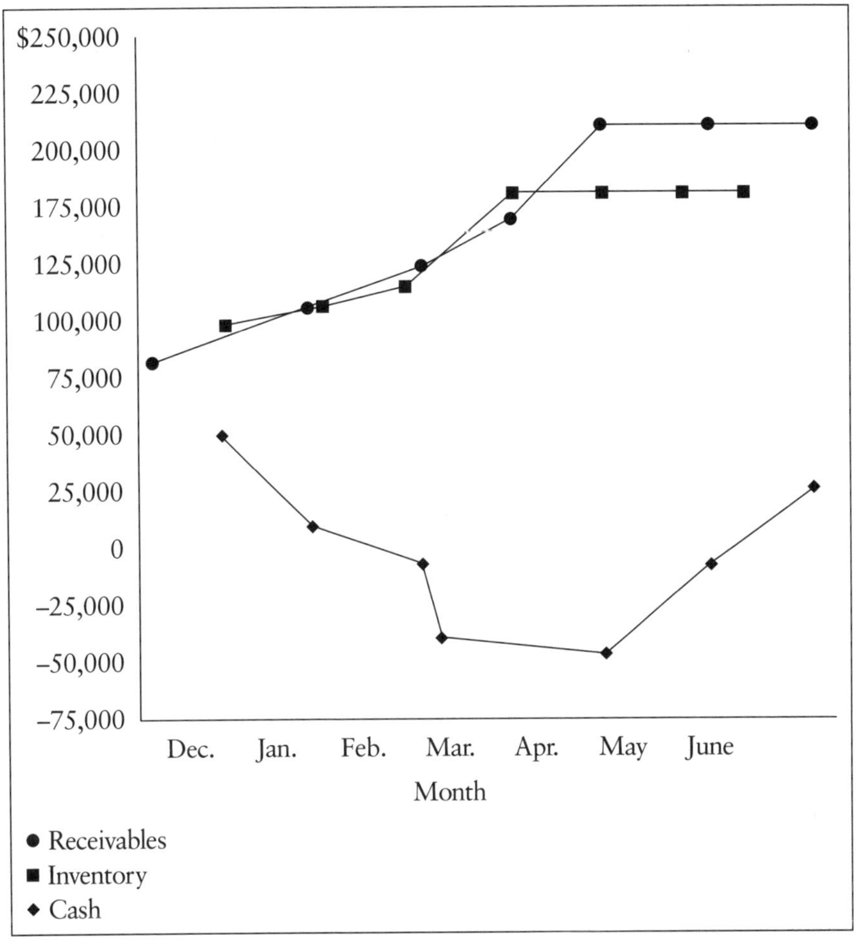

Figure 3.5. Cash flow trend.

extreme care to keep its financial house in order, such a cash flow can jeopardize the business's very existence. Growing too fast can be as hazardous as not growing at all. Many smaller companies believe that bigger means greater profit, but fast growth does not always mean larger profits. In their pursuit of growth, these companies often neglect existing customers, do not have the financial controls to handle growth, divert into new areas and encounter unanticipated problems, lack the necessary management skills, or wander away from their market niche and area of expertise.

CASH FLOW FORMULA

	Net profit
+	Depreciation
+	Increase in accounts payable
–	Increase in accounts receivable
–	Increase in inventory
–	Capital assets
	Cash flow

Positive cash flow factors include the following:

Slow sales growth	:	Less inventory/receivables
Shrinking sales	:	Less inventory/receivables
No new products	:	No research/development expense
Declining selling costs	:	Reduced expenses
Low inflation rate	:	Less working capital required
Low capital intensity	:	Less capital required
High market share	:	Reduced marketing expense
Steady market share	:	Reduced marketing expense

Negative cash flow factors include the following:

Rapid sales growth	:	Increased inventory/receivables
New products	:	Increased inventory/receivables
Increased sales growth	:	Increased inventory/receivables
High capital intensity	:	More capital required
Low market share	:	Increased marketing expenditures
Increasing market share	:	Increased marketing expenditures
High inflation rate	:	More working capital required

CREDIT MANAGEMENT

Many businesses put a tremendous effort into marketing and selling their products, while treating their credit and collection efforts as an afterthought.

Too great an investment in accounts receivable can hurt your business by tying up cash that could be used for other purposes. Many chief financial officers believe that credit and collections are more important than any other accounting function. A good way to measure the efficiency of your credit management is to compare your average collection period with that of your competitors or the industry average. If your average is higher, you may not be keeping sufficient control on the late payers, or your credit policy may be more liberal than others. If either is the case, you need to reconsider your credit program.

To emphasize the importance of this subject let us consider Table 3.1, which displays the effect of the collection period on accounts receivable. In perusing this table, one can see that the difference between collecting your receivables, in say, 30 days rather than 45 days is $41,096 for every $1,000,000 of credit sales. That is $41,096 of cash that you could have in the bank. For a business

Table 3.1. Receivables for annual credit sales.

		$1,000,000	$25,000,000	$50,000,000
Average collection period (days)	30	82,191	2,054,775	4,109,550
	35	95,890	2,397,250	4,794,500
	40	109,589	2,739,725	5,479,450
	45	123,287	3,082,175	6,164,350
	50	136,986	3,424,650	6,849,300
	55	150,684	3,767,100	7,534,200
	60	164,383	4,109,575	8,219,150

with $25,000,000 of revenue, that difference is $1,027,400. Would you rather have that amount of cash tied up in accounts receivable, or in the bank?

That decision is yours. The benefit is obvious. Paying extremely close attention to receivables should be the responsibility of the CEO and the CFO in a small or midsize business. They should review the aged accounts receivable detail at least twice monthly. In too many businesses this task is delegated to the billing staff, an action that can convey the impression that collecting the receivables are not a priority. Nothing could be further from the truth. If a business is short of cash, accounts receivable is the first place to look.

How do you compute the number of days of sales outstanding (DSO) in receivables? Very simply. The formula is as follows:

$$\frac{\text{Accounts receivable}}{\text{Annual credit sales/365 days}} = \text{DSO}$$

Example:

$$\frac{\$2{,}000{,}000 \text{ accounts receivable}}{\$16{,}000{,}000 \text{ annual sales/365 days}} = 46 \text{ days}$$

Now, assuming that you have to finance your receivables, consider Table 3.2, which displays your interest expense. For example, if your average days of sales outstanding are 45 days and you are paying 12% on your bank loans, then you are incurring $14,794 in annual interest expense to finance each $1,000,000 of annual credit sales. If your annual credit sales are $25,000,000, then in this example, your annual bill for interest would be $369,850. That is a lot of profit to give up.

Certainly you may need outside financing to be able to operate. However, do you need so much? Controlling your receivables and your inventory, as we will see later, can significantly free up cash and reduce your interest costs. It can also free up cash for expanding the business.

Table 3.2. $1,000,000 annual credit sales.

Interest rate	Annual interest costs for days of sales outstanding of:			
	30	45	60	90
8%	$ 6,575	$ 9,862	$13,150	$19,725
10%	8,219	12,328	16,438	24,656
12%	9,863	14,794	19,726	29,589
15%	12,328	18,492	24,656	36,984

For those businesses in the fortunate position of not having to borrow, the surplus funds generated could be invested.

Managing Accounts Receivable

Accounts receivable is often the largest asset that a business has. Yet many businesses manage their receivables very haphazardly. It pays to take the time to review your company's credit and collection procedures. You will only hurt your business by not doing so. Many businesses would not have cash flow problems if they just attempted to clean up their receivables management. The cash needs to be in your bank account, not your customers'. You cannot always be the "nice guy"; you are not in the banking business. Let somebody else finance them; you need to finance your own operation.

Dealing with receivables is not one of the more pleasant aspects of running a business. At times, in fact, it can be downright distasteful. However, it is a vital job that must be done, and it can be done well with certain controls and procedures:

- Perform credit checks on all new customers. This should be ongoing. You also need to run annual credit checks on those customers that comprise at least 80% of your business. For some larger and riskier customers, you may wish to review their credit status quarterly. Watch trade publications for news, both good and bad, about your customers. Seek pertinent trend information from trade associations that may foreshadow future problems with a customer.

- Provide credit only to those with good references.
- No credit should be accorded to potential deadbeats.
- No deliveries are made until credit is approved; deliveries must be cash up front until credit has been established.
- Set a credit limit for each customer. Do not exceed that prescribed limit. Inform sales reps when an account is near or at its credit limit.
- CEO/CFO approval should be necessary before providing further credit to those with past due balances.
- Pay sales commissions on the amount collected rather than on total sales generated. The sales reps might not like this, but they can understand that a sale is not complete until the goods are delivered and paid for. Commission "payment-upon-payment" provides an incentive for reps to sell to prompt-paying customers and use their influence to encourage their customers to stay current. They want to be paid too.
- Sell on shorter terms—for example, 30 days rather than 45 days of credit.
- Consider inducements, such as a 2% discount for prompt payment. Likewise, consider applying a finance charge for bills owed beyond a specific time, such as a penalty imposed after 30 or 45 days.
- Bankers talk to one another. Ask your banker to do a "credit check" in certain instances.
- Only the CEO or CFO can overrule the credit manager.
- Be careful in using credit as a sales tool. When business is slow, there is often the temptation to extend credit as an

inducement to purchase. Not allowing sales policy to influence credit policy is often best, if you wish to avoid bad debts and regrets later.

- Pay attention to invoicing. The secret of effective collections depends on efficient billing practices. It is amazing how many businesses are guilty of not submitting their invoices accurately or promptly. Inaccurate bills are a great excuse for customers to delay making payment. Many businesses also bill several days, if not a week or two, late. This is the first area to look at to speed up your collections. The sooner your customer has your invoice in hand, the sooner it will get into their payables system, and the sooner you will be paid. When I come across a business with a cash flow problem, often part of the problem lies with not getting invoices out and not following up on them.

Where the type of business permits it, invoices should be prepared and mailed the same day that delivery is made. In different circumstances, the invoice should be rendered at the first available opportunity.

Watch for early signs of trouble. Are customers suddenly taking longer to pay? Are they making partial or round sum payments, rather than paying a complete invoice or statement? How are they paying others? Has there been a sudden increase in their volume of purchases, indicating that they may have lost credit elsewhere? Many businesses wait too long when they suspect that an account is in trouble. All too often they get stuck, wishing to believe that the customer will resolve the difficulties.

Establish a formal system of collecting and follow it rigorously. Here is one way to do it:

1. Collection staff should call right away when the payment is not received on time. There is nothing to be gained by waiting.
2. At 15 days past due, the CFO should call the customer's counterpart.

3. At 30 days past due, the CEO should call the customer's counterpart.
4. Beyond this point, the account should be turned over to a collection agency or lawyer. All further sales or shipments should be strictly COD.

These measures may appear harsh; however, if somebody deals with you forthrightly they will not need to be implemented. Many businesses fear that they will lose a customer if they call and ask for payment. This is not true. Most such calls are handled initially by the bookkeeper or accounts payable clerk. It is not the most preposterous idea in the world that a company should get paid for its goods and services. You have kept your end of the bargain. Now it is time for your customer to keep its end.

- Hire a professional collector on staff, or designate a specific individual for the task. This is a tough job, and is not always suitable for "nice people." This position requires a person who is diligent and who has the communication skills, confidence, and perseverance to see matters resolved. Train the person well.
- Get feedback from your sales staff. They are often the first to know of a customer's difficulty.
- Use fax or express mail to get people's attention on past due accounts.

With the very small profit margins that businesses operate with today, it takes many new sales just to provide a sufficient margin to cover a bad debt. For example, a business with an operating profit of 2% that incurs a bad debt of $1000 has to produce $50,000 of sales just to cover that bad debt!

LOST REVENUE

There is hardly a business in existence selling on credit that does not lose revenue due to problems with its billing function. A billing clerk may fall behind in billing and seek to cover up the problem by perpetuating it. Or, there may be a loophole or missing link in the billing system that has gone unnoticed. Systems are not always perfect; do not assume that all billings go out. Or, somebody could be withholding information from the system. Whatever the nature of your particular business, I urge you to review your entire billing function without delay. If necessary, you may find it useful to seek the opinion of your public accounting firm. It will be worth the effort.

INVENTORY

Inventory represents a substantial cash investment for most businesses and must be well managed to maximize profits. In a manufacturing firm, it can represent 30% of total assets. In wholesale and retail firms, inventory may represent 60% or more of all assets.

This area, when properly managed, can often yield very significant cash benefits. Management often does not concern itself with inventory, primarily because of the mind-boggling detail associated with monitoring it.

Unless inventories are monitored and controlled, they can prove very costly in terms of expense and wastage. Inventory is an expensive and somewhat risky form of an asset. Storage, handling, obsolescence, insurance, financing, and shrinkage costs all eat into operating margins. Many business owners fail to appreciate the true cost of carrying inventory. The total annual cost may amount to 15% to 25%. When inventory gets out of hand, it drains away cash and ultimately produces markdowns.

Many consider inventory the most difficult resource to control. Those who are responsible for it prefer to err on the side of caution, for the last thing that they want to be accused of is running out of a particular item. They would prefer to maintain too much inventory rather than be caught short.

The purchasing manager or those responsible for inventory levels are usually hit with a barrage of contradictory instructions. Do you recognize any of the following in your business?

- "Maintain a variety of inventory—but do not run too low on the more popular items."
- "Reduce inventory levels to increase inventory turnover rates—but do not run out of anything."
- "Buy in bulk to achieve price breaks—but do not carry any slow-moving inventory."
- "Always have a sufficient level of inventory on hand—but please, no obsolete items."

Managing Inventory

The best cash flow will result from an inventory level that:

- Prevents excessive stock-outs
- Allows for growth
- Enables satisfactory customer service
- Facilitates a smooth production schedule

It is very important to monitor how often inventory turns over during a year. If a business with an annual cost of goods sold of $1,000,000 has an inventory level of $500,000, it is only turning over inventory twice a year. Were it to reduce that inventory to, say, $150,000, it will have greatly increased its turnover rate, and in the process will have freed up $350,000 of cash. Business today is realizing significant cash savings through improved inventory management.

It is, thus, very important to monitor your inventory turnover rate. The formula is:

$$\frac{\text{Current inventory}}{\text{Annual cost of sales/365 days}} = \text{Days on hand}$$

Examples:

$$\frac{\text{Economy line: } \$100{,}000}{\$1{,}825{,}000/365} = 20 \text{ days}$$

$$\frac{\text{Standard line: } \$180{,}000}{\$2{,}265{,}555/365} = 29 \text{ days}$$

$$\frac{\text{Deluxe line: } \$130{,}000}{\$1{,}825{,}000/365} = 26 \text{ days}$$

This approach provides a rough guideline by which management can set goals to improve performance.

It is important to compare your inventory turnover rate with the industry norm. If your rate is lower, you may be unnecessarily tying up cash or holding onto obsolete items. Perhaps for competitive purposes you carry a full range of inventory, including items in low demand. Whatever the case, if you have excess inventory, it is time to reevaluate your inventory policy.

Manufacturing concerns should look closely at the length of time it takes to get inventory from receipt to distribution. The longer the throughput time, the more work-in-process inventory sits around awaiting action. Speeding up the process will serve to eliminate excess inventory needs and will free up cash.

Effective inventory management requires an understanding of:

- The sales history of each product and product line
- The seasonal factors involved
- The turnover rates of key product lines
- How low you can allow the inventory of each product to go without undue risk of stock-out
- How much you should reorder

- What products or lines can be eliminated, thereby giving you greater buying power with those that remain
- What products have the best margins
- What you can do to increase the turnover of high-margin products.

The finance staff should be involved in purchasing planning to coordinate inventory buying and cash flow. Don't be a slave to the numbers, but let them serve as a guide. Remember, the past is not necessarily the best predictor of the future. Needs, styles, and trends change. The marketplace is a dynamic and ever-changing entity. Get input from those who are closest to it—your sales and marketing people. Don't forget that other valued source of information—your customers!

Inventory Danger Signs

- Inventories are rising faster than sales.
- Large differences arise between actual inventory and accounting records.
- Write-offs of obsolete inventory items are increasing.
- Frequent customer complaints are received about backorders and missed deliveries.
- Interruption of production schedules is often necessary to expedite specific orders.
- Inventory turnover is generally below average for the industry.

Inventory Management Systems

Good inventory management has become increasingly critical in recent years. The improvement of inventory management requires systems that simplify improved decision making. Start by identifying the 20 most frequently handled and expensive items in your inventory. Using a computerized graphing program, set up a separate graph for each item. For an example, see Figure 3.6. Studying the figure, with use running at about 250 units per week, a serious overstock position occurred in weeks 1 through 4. An average inventory was being carried in that period of 600 units, or nearly two-and-a-half-weeks' supply. As the supplier appears to be able to restock within a short time frame, there does not appear to be a need to carry such a large inventory. Starting in week 5, inventory was brought down to a more appropriate level.

Using such a graph can pinpoint the cause of inventory imbalance and permit improved control over inventory levels. The graph will answer such crucial questions as how much of each item you should keep on hand and the size and frequency of reorders. A reliable supplier can help you reduce the volume of goods on hand while still maintaining an adequate level.

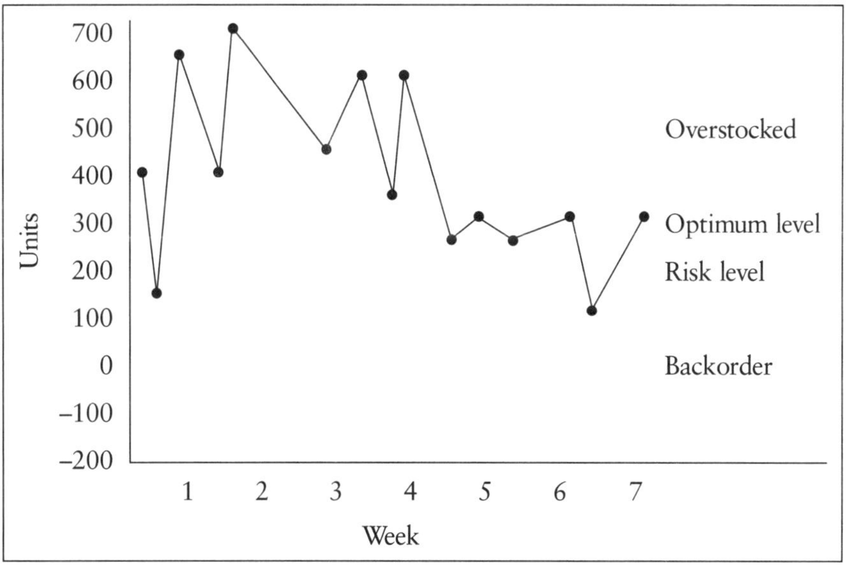

Figure 3.6. Graph that will assist with inventory management.

The solution to most inventory problems is the establishment of an order entry system that matches up orders, inventory, and production schedules by product code.

MORE SUGGESTIONS TO IMPROVE CASH FLOW

Other than the previous points regarding the management of accounts receivable and inventory, some specific suggestions to improve cash flow are:

- Convert the payroll to biweekly from weekly if this has not been done already. The changeover can be phased in to prevent hardships.
- Use a letter of credit in lieu of cash when making any large rent or other deposits.
- Manage accounts payable more closely to conserve cash. Vendor financing is important for any business, and especially so if you can sell the inventory item before having to pay the vendor.
- Cut your expenses. This is a crucial element for general business viability, a healthier cash flow, and impact on profitability.
- Sell slow-moving inventory at a discount. Sacrificing profits for cash flow is sometimes necessary.
- For a business in a perpetually tight cash situation, a sale and leaseback of assets can help. Such businesses should avoid increasing sales, as doing so boosts inventory and receivables to the detriment of cash flow.

TROUBLED BUSINESSES

For businesses in financial difficulty, the first thing to do is to focus on cash flow. With the necessary cash you can make your payroll and pay the important vendors. Focus on getting the billing out, turning over inventory, collecting receivables, eliminating unnecessary expenditures, and checking your profit margins.

SUMMARY

In many businesses, cash flow is an alien concept. The owners or management focus only on sales and profits. Why should they think differently? Very simply, because cash is the lifeblood of a business. You cannot be in control if your cash flow is out of control.

Most entrepreneurs and business managers are sales driven. They think that if sales are rising, everything else will take care of itself. They forget the impact of the rising receivables and inventory. Then one day, without warning—or so they say—they find that there is no cash available to make the payroll or to pay the suppliers. Cash flow mismanagement is an insidious affliction and killer of many businesses.

Cash flow consciousness should pervade all business thinking and decision making. Everyone in your company—from the purchasing managers to the production managers on down to the sales staff and the credit and collection staff—should operate with a cash flow consciousness. It should play an ever-present part in everyone's decision making.

If life is a journey and business an adventure, envision yourself on a canoe trip. Profitability is the river you are navigating, but cash flow is the current that runs through it. With a good strong current carrying you along, your trip is that much easier.

4 Price Right to Profit

Other than revenue growth and expense control, probably no other aspect of your business offers the opportunity to enhance profits as does pricing correctly. It is not the customer's responsibility to see to it that you make a profit. That is up to you.

Pricing is both an art and a game. It is usually a function of what the market will bear and what your competitors charge. Often it is a response to competitive pressures and an effort to influence competitors' pricing behavior.

Unfortunately, not all businesses are as organized in this area as one might expect. An inability to grasp pricing is often a cause of financial difficulty. Many have no real pricing strategy other than the three shoot-from-the-hip approaches commonly used.

- *Cost-plus pricing.* Many businesses do not know their true costs in the first place, so how they use this approach is difficult to comprehend. Further, it takes no account of competitive behavior or customer responses.
- *Matching your competitor's price.* This is better known as the blind leading the blind. Since there is a good chance that your competitors do not know their true costs and may have relied on guesswork to establish their prices, where does that leave you?

- *Russian roulette pricing.* This is where you simply decide to undercut your competition. Period. Knowing how much thought they may have given to setting their prices, this approach could be equivalent to playing Russian roulette.

A frequent mistake made by businesses is allowing their marketing and sales staff to set prices. There is something of an inherent conflict of interest in allowing this, since their mission is to sell, not to maximize revenue. Give them a profit margin by product or department if you wish, and they can then work within that parameter when dealing with individual customers. You should certainly seek their consultation in setting prices, but do not delegate the entire responsibility to them.

In establishing prices, there are four fundamental questions that you must consider.

- What is our pricing strategy, and how did we arrive at it?
- What are our costs, and how were they determined?
- What impact will our pricing decisions have on our customers, both in the short term and the long term? Will they be attracted or scared away?
- Where will our competitors price?

Pricing strategies vary greatly by type of industry. Some traditional strategies include the following:

- *Cost-based pricing.* This approach assumes that you can accurately identify your true costs. If your costs are not competitive, this approach can lead to major problems. No business can be guaranteed a profit.
- *Target pricing.* Designed to produce a specific return on sales or on invested capital.
- *Skimming pricing.* Here you enter the market with a high price on a new product before it becomes necessary to lower it as competition appears.

- *Penetration pricing.* Where a potentially large market exists and competition is expected, using economies of scale in production and marketing, a low price is set to penetrate the market quickly.
- *Predatory pricing.* Pricing set to hold off or drive away competition.
- *Prestige pricing.* This refers to setting a high price on an item to suggest status or high quality. To some, a higher price signals that the product is of high quality.

In deciding on your strategy, you must first determine what pricing objective you wish to achieve:

- Maximize profits.
- Maintain or increase your market share.
- Maintain the status quo with the competition and the marketplace.
- Any combination of these.

Then, conduct customer research to determine the real value that customers place on your product. Ascertain how each market segment defines quality and what attracts them to your product rather than your competitors' product. Surveying your competitors' customers is important also, as well as your former customers who have switched their allegiance, to understand why they do not favor your product. Learn from the problems revealed by the survey, understand why they occurred, and then correct them.

Based on the data collected regarding customers' perception of value and on sales history, you can project the volume that is likely to be sold at various price levels. You need then to project the costs, revenue, and profit margin at each volume/price level.

You are then at a point where you can choose a price that will allow the business to achieve its objectives.

SETTING YOUR PRICES

The following discussions and examples relate mainly to a manufacturing enterprise and to retail and certain service businesses. However, much of the same approach and principles also apply to other service businesses.

Whatever your particular pricing strategy, the first step is to understand the basic formula that produces a profit.

	Unit sales price
–	Product cost
–	Variable cost
	Profit margin
×	Sales volume
	Total profit margin
–	Overhead expense
	Operating profit before taxes

Unit sales price is what you sell an item for. Product cost is the direct cost of the materials related to the item. Variable cost is generally the labor and plant cost related to producing the item. (For the sake of simplicity, we are not recognizing reductions in variable costs as a result of increases in volume.)

When you do not have the luxury of cost accountants on your staff, how do you determine these unit costs? You should approach the question by product line. To determine your product cost, total the cost of all materials used to produce the product and divide your answer by the total number of units produced.

Determining your per-unit variable cost can be more difficult, as you may well produce more than one line of products. There are two steps to producing the result. For the labor cost, if certain employees work only with a particular line, then this should be simple enough to determine. If employees work on more than one product line, then you will need to perform a time study to determine the time appropriate to each line. In either case, divide your result by the total line production. To determine the plant cost, you can use two approaches. You can either prorate these costs using total units produced for all lines as the denominator, or the square footage occupied in the production of each line as a percentage of total square footage occupied multiplied by the total space cost. Divide your answer by the total line production.

Now let us apply some numbers to all of this theory. Let us take the example of the Widget Company. The relevant data for their economy line is as follows:

Sales price per unit	$ 100
Product cost	45
Variable cost	15
Annual sales volume	8000 units
Overhead expense	$260,000

Applying these data to the formula, we find:

Unit sales price	$100
Unit product cost	<45>
Unit variable cost	<15>
Profit margin	40
× Sales volume	8000 units
Total profit margin	320,000
– Overhead expense	<260,000>
Operating profit before taxes	$ 60,000

The profit margin is the sales price less the product and variable costs. You therefore start by setting your sales price, and presumably control your product and variable costs to maximize your profit margin.

For all of this to work, you need to meet your sales volume goals, in order to produce the total profit margin necessary to cover your lean and trim overhead expenses and to produce an appropriate operating profit result.

Were your internal or external accountants producing an income statement for you from the data, it would likely read more like the following:

Total sales		$ 800,000
Product cost	$360,000	
Variable costs	$120,000	<480,000>
Total profit margin		320,000
Overhead expenses		<260,000>
Operating profit		$ 60,000

Such as income statement tells you that you made a profit, but it does not really tell you *how* you made that profit. You need to understand the underlying economics—what does it cost to produce parts, for labor, for distribution? How does the selling price compare with what the market will bear? Financial statements bring all of these facts together into one group of numbers without providing the detail you need.

The formula used here provides much information useful to management, such as:

- Sales volume
- Per-unit costs
- Profit margin per unit

It also enables you to quickly calculate your break-even point, as we shall now see.

BREAK-EVEN ANALYSIS

Break-even analysis means determining the point at which revenue equals the production and overhead costs at a given price. It requires dividing the overhead expense by the profit margin per unit. Thus, from our example,

$$\frac{\text{Overhead expense: \$260,000}}{\text{Profit margin per unit: \$40}} = 6500 \text{ units}$$

Therefore, the Widget Company has to sell 6500 units of the economy line before it breaks even on the line. Since it sold 8000 units, the 1500 units above the break-even point, when multiplied by the $40 profit margin per unit, produced the $60,000 operating profit.

If you have not already done so, you need to complete this exercise for each product or service line in your business.

For the sake of simplicity, this particular break-even compilation assumes that the product and variable costs are constant. This is not always the case, as such costs usually rise in line with inflationary pressures, and can rise and fall in line with changes in volume.

Break-even analysis is more of a management tool for monitoring and evaluating the business than for establishing prices, although it can be applied there as well.

SALES VOLUME AND PRICE CHANGES

Let us consider a number of scenarios and the resulting effect on operating profit.

A 10% Sales Volume Increase

Sales volume would rise in our example to 8800 units from 8000 units. The profit margin per unit would not be affected and would remain at $40, as the product and variable costs would change in tandem with the volume changes. Thus, the revised situation would read:

	Profit margin per unit	$ 40
×	Sales volume	8800 units
=	Total profit margin	$ 352,000
	Overhead expenses	260,000
	Operating profit	$ 92,000

Operating profit increases by $32,000, which is represented by the 800 additional units sold times the $40 profit margin per unit. Since only sales volume changed and overhead expense remained constant, the entire $32,000 of additional profit margin flowed directly to the bottom line.

Increasing your sales volume can obviously be very beneficial for your business. Overhead expenses usually do not rise incrementally with increases in sales volume—at least they shouldn't!

A 10% Sales Volume Decrease

Sales volume would thus drop from 8000 units to 7200 units:

	Profit margin per unit	$ 40
×	Sales volume	7200 units
=	Total profit margin	$ 288,000
	Overhead expenses	260,000
	Operating profit	$ 28,000

Operating profit thus falls by $32,000, which is the profit margin on the 800 units dropped. If this trend were not reversed, attention would need to be focused on reducing the overhead expense to bring it in line with the reduced sales volume.

In both instances where sales volume changed by 10%, the percentage effect on the bottom line was more dramatic. In the case of the 10% sales volume increase, operating profit increased from $60,000 to $92,000 for a gain of 53%. Similarly, in the case of the 10% sales volume decrease, the operating profit dropped from $60,000 to $28,000—a change of 53% in the other direction.

In both instances the overhead expense remained constant; thus, the change in total profit margin directly impacted the bottom line. What can we learn from these two examples?

1. How important sales volume is in ensuring the profitability of a business
2. How beneficial an increase in sales volume can be

As many businesses have found, sales volume is of paramount importance. The less you charge, the more you'll earn as reduced prices expand the market's size—up to a point. However, as we shall see later, do your arithmetic before reducing prices, or you could find yourself actually losing money.

A 10% Sales Price Increase

Such an increase would raise the per-unit sales price in our example to $110. All other factors would remain the same. Thus,

	Unit sales price	$ 110
	Unit product cost	<45>
	Unit variable cost	<15>
	Profit margin	$ 50
×	Sales volume	8000 units
=	Total profit margin	$ 400,000
	Overhead expense	<260,000>
	Operating profit	$ 140,000

The operating profit increases from \$60,000 to \$140,000, or a gain of \$80,000 (133%). The \$10 per unit increase in price flows directly to the bottom line. Product and variable cost are not affected; neither is overhead expense.

The break-even point is further reduced also.

$$\frac{\text{Overhead expense: \$260,000}}{\text{Profit margin per unit: \$50}} = \text{5200 units}$$

Therefore, with a 10% sales price increase, the break-even point drops by 20% to 5200 units.

Now, before you decide to raise your prices by 10% tomorrow morning, please remember that we are only dealing with a hypothetical situation here. Before you raise your prices to any extent, you must first consider the impact on your customers and your competition. Generally, as prices go up, demand goes down. Customers do without, or stick with their old product. To obtain a higher price, you often need to provide something different or a value-added feature or service that no one else is providing. It might be enhancing the quality of your product or service, or further improving your service level to customers. Without a doubt, customers are the most important party to consider in pricing. Even businesses that price on a cost-plus basis have to be concerned with customer acceptance. In establishing prices, you need to know how much elasticity there is in the demand for the product or service. In the case of a patient requiring emergency medical care, there is plenty of elasticity there in setting a price for the treatment, whereas a couple contemplating a weekend getaway will be inelastic when considering how much they will pay for air fare or a package deal.

Through market research and price experimentation, you need to establish the optimum price for your product or service. You should establish the appropriate price level for each customer or customer group, then design a price-appropriate product or service for each.

Some businesses take the "cram-down" approach when setting their prices. They decide what customers want and how much they will have to pay. This is a quick way to go broke.

In your zeal to maximize profits and establish your optimum price levels, bear in mind that you must constantly assess the best relative price for your products. Setting prices is not a one-time effort. If you are to avoid reacting to the marketplace, you must monitor your price levels on an ongoing basis to ensure that your present and future customers will continue to choose your service or product.

While you certainly should seek to maximize pricing and profits, you must also be wary of pricing yourself out of business or of creating an opportunity for the competition. The French wine industry in 1993 illustrated a classic market mechanism when the price of higher-quality wines took a dive. Consumers revolted when the product became too expensive, and they could only be induced to return when prices became affordable or "reasonable" once again. Continuous annual increases in the volume of wine sold, matched by constant price increases, led the industry to believe that this pattern could go on forever. When consumers balked and switched to cheaper wines, it took the producers some time to understand and accept that they had overpriced their product.

The pursuit of premium pricing always creates an opportunity for your competitors. In this example, the other wineries of the world were the beneficiaries. Charging what the market will bear sounds good, but you could also be opening up a risk-free opportunity for your competition.

Premium pricing, and its resulting high profit margins, do not of themselves create maximum profits. Profit is the factor of your volume times your profit margin. Maximum profit is not the profit margin that produces the greatest volume, as this would be a price close to zero dollars where everyone would want to buy. Inversely, the highest profit will not usually be derived from that single customer foolish enough to pay a significant premium. Maximum profit is derived from the profit margin that produces the largest total profit flow, which is usually the profit margin that produces the greatest market share.

Sharp reductions in the price for personal computers opened up a vast new consumer market that continues to grow. Until Microsoft became a software force, personal computing was beyond the means of many consumers because of high prices. Microsoft understood that prices had to come down before consumers would get interested, and in that regard, marketing and pricing are just as important as product quality.

It happens that when squeezed for profit, some businesses instinctively respond by raising prices. Raising prices frequently just reduces the customer base, reducing market share. When too many businesses in the same industry raise prices, the result is usually a smaller market, as consumers make do with less.

When price increases do not achieve the desired bottom-line effect, some businesses addictively just raise prices again. But trying to squeeze out more profits with higher prices just serves to squeeze out even more customers. You only need to look at the airline industry as an example. When the airlines raise prices, discretionary travelers stay home. When airlines such as Southwest offer reduced fares they significantly expand the size of their market, as a larger segment of the market can afford to take to the skies. With enhanced volume, price reductions—not price increases—can be the road to greater profits.

As noted earlier, lower costs lead to lower prices, which in turn lead to greater volume. This leads to even lower costs, which in turn lead to still lower prices. And so the cycle continues.

Another factor that you must consider is the response of competitors to any price change you make. If you raise prices, will they match your increase or a portion thereof, or will they hold their price level and seek to pick up your customers? Conversely, if you lower prices, will they:

1. Also cut their prices?
2. Go even lower than you did?
3. Or keep their prices as they are?

What all of this tells us is that you must consider the needs and wants of others. You cannot operate in a vacuum when making pricing decisions, and you must try to project as best you can the consequences of your actions. However, you must never be afraid to set your prices at a level sufficient to achieve a reasonable profit. Profit, after all, is the ultimate reason for the business's existence.

A 10% Sales Price Decrease

Suppose in seeking to gain additional market share, or to turn around a loss-making situation by increasing the sales unit volume, you decide to drop your prices 10%. What would the impact be? In this example, the effect is not very good if it is a permanent price reduction. The unit sales price would drop to $90. Thus,

	Unit sales price	$ 90
	Unit product cost	<45>
	Unit variable cost	<15>
	Profit margin	$ 30
×	Sales volume	8000 units
=	Total profit margin	240,000
	Overhead expense	<260,000>
	Operating loss	$ 20,000

The break-even point here would be:

$$\frac{\text{Overhead expense: \$260,000}}{\text{Profit margin: \$30}} = 8666 \text{ units}$$

To break even, therefore, the business would have to increase its sales volume by 666 units or 8.3%. Remember, that is only to break even. To maintain its operating profit at $60,000, the business would have to sell 2000 more units ($60,000 divided by $30 profit margin) for a total sales volume of 10,666 units, or an increase of 33%. You need to ask yourself how realistic such a sales volume increase would be.

The foregoing assumes, of course, that the price decrease is permanent. Even if it isn't, you have to consider what you hope to gain by such a move, as price advantages are usually short-lived. Most likely your competitors will match your move, so a price cut often means that competitors maintain their market shares at lower price levels. However, it could work as a loss leader to attract attention to your other products, create a generalized low-price image, or—on the premise that demand for a product tends to increase as the price is lowered—you may increase your volume. A price cut can also be beneficial if it helps you dispose of slow-moving inventory and convert it to cash.

While many business owners understand that a price war can eliminate profits in the short term, they often fail to realize the long-term damage. Customer perceptions about what constitutes acceptable prices are not short-lived. Rather, their idea about the right price for a product or service remains long after a price war. Customers often hold off on making purchases until they see a return to the price war level. No one wins a price war. You try to hang on and survive. Usually you end up exchanging customers at lower margins.

With the low operating profit levels that prevail today, even a 1% drop in prices for a business with a 5% profit margin can result in a 20% drop in profits, assuming no increase in volume.

Overall, a sales price increase is more beneficial to the bottom line than a sales volume increase of the same percentage. With the latter, the product and variable costs have to be covered first before a benefit shows up in operating profit, whereas a sales price increase goes directly to the bottom line in its entirety. For example, if a business producing an operating profit of 5% on sales increased its prices by 1%, the result would be an operating profit of 6%, or a gain of 20% to the bottom line. Since so many businesses operate with low operating profit percentages in today's competitive environment, a small sales price increase can have a dramatic impact. If a business producing a 2% operating profit raises its prices by 2% without a loss of volume, it doubles its operating profit. However, if this business reduces its expenses by 2%, it also doubles its operating profit! This is something to think about.

This is all fine in theory, but before you make any such moves, first consider the reaction of your customers and your competition.

A 10% Sales Price Decrease with an Offsetting ?% Sales Volume Increase

In an effort to boost sales and fill up some idle capacity, you decide to cut prices by 10% to stimulate demand and increase volume. As we saw earlier, a larger increase in sales volume is required to offset a smaller percentage decrease in sales prices, because of the need to cover the product and variable costs. How do you determine what the sales volume increase should be to offset such a price decrease? Using this example as a basis for the decision.

Step 1: A 10% sales price decrease would produce a gross sales reduction of $80,000.

Step 2: The profit margin per unit would now be $30.

Step 3: Divide $80,000 by $30 to determine the additional unit sales necessary. The result is 2666 units, or a 33% increase.

The obvious question is: How feasible is a sales volume gain of that magnitude? Probably not very feasible. Depending on the type of business, a 10% price cut would not often stimulate that type of additional demand. On the other hand, such a price cuts would bring an avalanche of business for someone like an automobile dealer, but at the same time it would leave them broke, given the slim profit margins in percentage terms. As Lee Iacocca has said, "Volume times zero isn't too healthy." Once again, you need to very carefully consider the various impacts of any price changes.

A 5% Sales Price Increase, with an Offsetting ?% Sales Volume Decrease

Since sales volume often moves in the opposite direction of sales price increases, we are seeking to determine how much of a sales volume loss one could take without sacrificing any operating profit to a price increase. Obviously one's logic and business skills would have to be seriously flawed to plan on dropping profits as the result of a price increase. The purpose of this exercise is to stimulate thought for when you actually may plan an increase.

A 5% sales price increase would result in raising prices in our example by $5 per unit.

Step 1: The profit margin would increase to $45.

Step 2: For the total profit margin to remain at $320,000 and operating profit at $60,000, the business would have to sell 7111 units ($320,000 divided by $45).

Step 3: 7111 units represent an 11% drop from the previous level of 8000 units.

Keep in mind that overhead expenses remained constant, thus we only had to focus on profit margin to determine the impact of the price and volume changes.

In this example, the business could "afford" to lose 11% of its sales volume with a 5% price increase and still produce the same operating profit. Of course, one should not plan on losing any customers if at all possible.

Price increases should generally be the result of inflationary pressures or enhanced quality in your product or service that supports and justifies the increase. For reasons other than these, raising prices to cover increased overhead expense or to produce a larger operating profit is not always a good idea. High prices are like drugs—they hook you. Your competitors gain an advantage on you, and you run the risk of shrinking your market share through pricing yourself out of the range of some customers. Improving productivity and/or reducing expenses is a much better approach, as is increasing your sales volume. As we shall see later in this book, the key to success for many businesses is volume and aggressive marketing. Coupled with tight control on expenses, this is the best way to grow your profits.

PRODUCT LINE PROFIT PICTURE

Quite often we hear the saying that 20% of our products or services yield 80% of the profit. This is often very true. I have seen a number of businesses that were producing healthy operating profits where the entire bottom line was derived from a single product line or segment of the business. Because the businesses overall were quite profitable, nobody ever concerned themselves with looking at the details or contribution of each line.

Let us take an example of a somewhat unhealthy business.

	Product Line			
	Economy	Standard	Deluxe	Average/ Total
Sales price	$100	$105	$110	$105
Product cost	<45>	<54>	<63>	<54>
Variable cost	<15>	<18>	<21>	<18>
Profit margin	40	33	26	33
Sales volume: units	8,000	10,000	12,000	30,000
Gross sales	$800,000	$1,050,000	$1,320,000	$3,170,000
Total profit margin	320,000	330,000	312,000	962,000
Overhead expense	<260,000>	<325,000>	<390,000>	<975,000>

Operating profit/<loss>	60,000	5,000	<78,000>	<13,000>
Gross profit %	40	31	24	31
Sales volume %	25	33	42	100
Operating profit/<loss> %	7.5	0.5	<5.9>	<0.4>

Overhead expense in this example is allocated based on sales volume. A good argument can be made for allocating it according to the total direct costs for each line. Were we to do this, the product line profit picture would look even more bleak for the deluxe line.

Operating profit/<loss>	
Economy	$ 108,044
Standard	12,066
Deluxe	<133,110>
Operating loss	<13,000>

The facts in this presentation are not as bizarre or exaggerated as you might think. Many businesses find themselves in this position. The lesson to be learned from this? Break down your operating profit by product/service line.

Clearly, there is a major problem with the pricing of the standard and deluxe lines. Higher-quality products generally have higher profit margins. This is not the case here, which exemplifies a common mistake that businesses make in not seeking a premium price for a new or higher-quality product. Where a business does not charge a higher price for a premium product or greater benefits, competitors are forced to lower their prices to remain competitive. Where you are the competitor to a business that is mispricing its products, this is a problem.

It is quite apparent that management has never previously attempted to develop data on the profitability of each line. Had they done so, the operating results would be a lot different. Quite likely they assumed that the product and variable costs bore only a slight differentiation by line, when in fact there were sizable differences.

In this instance, management is now faced with the difficult task of significantly raising prices on the standard and deluxe lines. The economy line is producing an operating profit of 7.5%, which is probably quite reasonable. Producing a similar percentage on the other two lines would necessitate price increases of 7.6% and 14.5%, respectively. In the real world it might be difficult to enact such price increases, especially on the deluxe line.

How to do it? As a first step, a promotional campaign highlighting the attributes and quality of these lines should be initiated. The more consumers value the quality and unique attributes that separate a product from competing products, the less sensitive they are to price. Consumers understand price dynamics. They understand that they have to pay a premium price to obtain premium value. When they understand the price-versus-value decision, the majority goes for value. But first the value must be explained to them—both the customer service and the attributes of the product. Give them the added reasons, the perceived value, and they will pay a little more.

The business that operates on price alone will get its share of customers. You cannot prevent that. But you can retain your market share by differentiating yourself from the price merchants through offering the perceived value. The most effective way to differentiate your business is to provide service that's better than what your competitors offer and more than what the customers expect.

In today's world where all services and products are virtually alike, superior customer service is the one sure way to differentiate yourself from the competition. The connection with a customer does not end with the transaction. That's just the beginning. Your superior service and quality must be the inducement to keep them returning.

INCREMENTAL COST PRICING

Incremental cost pricing means establishing a price on the basis of direct costs only. This approach is used by airlines to fill empty seats through supersaver fares and by manufacturers under special circumstances, such as unused capacity, depressed business conditions, or selling outside of the normal market. An unusually large order might be accepted at a price sufficient to cover direct labor and material costs, with a small amount left over to contribute to overhead. Such sales may be made to keep a labor force intact during a slow period, and to avoid the cost of a shutdown.

Discounts to dispose of end-of-season merchandise or to sell a large ticket item such as an automobile, household appliances, or furnishings are common. Provided that the price is more than sufficient to cover the basic cost of the service or merchandise plus any direct costs attributable to the item, plus making a contribution to overhead, the business is better off than it would be in losing the sale. Such reasoning assumes, of course, that the business has a stream of normal-price business sufficient in volume to cover its operating expenses and to produce a profit. A danger is that the practice of discounting prices may lead all customers to expect to pay a price that only covers direct variable costs.

Airlines are an example of such a pricing strategy. Nearly 90% of passengers travel at some level of a discount, some at a substantial discount. The marginal cost of flying an extra passenger—meals, extra fuel burned, and sales commission on the ticket—is less than one-fourth the cost of a full price ticket. Therefore an airline eager to sell empty seats can rationalize a deep discount, provided that the extra passengers cover (with a little to spare) the low marginal costs of boarding them.

Incremental pricing in a limited number of situations can have a benefit, as long as you don't make a habit of it.

ONE-PRICE POLICY VERSUS A VARYING PRICE POLICY

A one-price policy, or a policy of uniform selling prices, requires that the same price be charged to all customers. Such a policy, however, does not prevent one from changing prices as frequently as desired, provided that all customers are charged the same price at any given time. A one-price policy is characteristic of most retail firms. Retailers dealing with large numbers of customers, such as department stores or supermarkets, find such a policy to be essential.

With a varying price policy, discounts or price concessions are given to certain important customers or because of the competitive environment or a customer's bargaining ability. Concessions can take many forms, such as a lower price quotation, extra trade or cash discounts, or discounts for very large quantities.

Manufacturers and wholesalers do not commonly adhere to a one-price policy. Many consumers and dealers like to bargain and to realize savings from a transaction. A varying price policy gives a salesperson leeway to quote prices, within established limits, to meet competition on a price basis.

Because of the large quantities involved, and the small gross margins on which purchasers operate in the wholesale field, slight changes in prices may mean the difference between a profit or loss on a transaction.

SUMMARY

Whatever your line of business, and whatever your pricing policy, there is one cardinal rule: Know your true costs. It is sad to consider the number of businesses that think they know their true costs, but in fact do not. Know your true costs for each item or product that you sell. Your company's well-being depends on it.

Price right to profit. Know where your profits are coming from.

5 Each Customer Is an Annuity

Goodwill is the one and only asset that competition cannot undersell or destroy.

—Marshall Field

Each customer should be viewed as an annuity, providing a continuous stream of revenue. You must do everything you can to not pollute that stream. Treat each customer as you would any revenue-producing asset. Many businesses have now come to the realization that their customers are their most valuable asset. In addition, they also now realize that customers are their most underutilized asset.

A study conducted by the Strategic Planning Institute in Cambridge, Massachusetts, found that:

- The better service performers charge about 9% more for their goods.
- Their sales grow twice as fast, 17% versus 8%; they increase their market share by 6% a year, while the poor performers lose 2% a year.
- The service stars earn a 12% return on sales, versus a measly 1% for the others.

Considering this, and the fact that it can cost five times more to recruit a new customer than to retain an existing customer, any company that does not strive for superb customer service is setting itself up for trouble. Good customer service is good business. Customer service is an integral part of your product. In some businesses, it *is* your product. It's the humanizing factor that can distinguish you from the competition and help you build and retain a base of satisfied customers. Never forget that you are in business to satisfy your customers' needs. Success is derived from focusing on the customer.

Just consider the annuity value of existing customers:

- You serve these accounts for many years without the marketing and advertising recruitment cost of getting a new customer.
- The size of their orders increase as they grow, which increases your profits.
- They recommend you to others, who also become long-term customers; this further increases your profits.

The problem with many profitable businesses is convincing decision makers to change their thinking. If their ethic or outlook is short term—that is, on maximizing profits—there is little chance that they will change to focus on those aspects of the business necessary for long-term success such as superb customer service and product quality. This is too bad, for they are jeopardizing the future well-being of the business. Investing in these areas now may or may not increase or maximize profits, but will help to maintain those profits.

Businesses that fail to delight their customers are playing Russian roulette with their very survival. In today's competitive market where there are more sellers than ever before, businesses must find ways to give customers more value than just the product itself.

There's an old adage that the customer is not just buying the product, but also buying the salesperson. Why? Because of the service, the satisfaction and comfort level, and the feeling of being respected, responded to, and appreciated. Salesmanship today is essentially customer service, and vice versa.

Service has reached this level of importance today due to such factors as global trade competition, changing lifestyles, and the impact of technology. The increasing importance of customer expectations regarding service has strong implications for the small business. It is the one inexpensive yet priceless way for the small business to distinguish itself from the competition.

Customers expect the small business to be close to them and to offer an extra touch of personal, caring service. The best attitude to have is: Although you are a separate company, you are a vital and intimate part of your customer's business; a kind of outsider, yet insider, relationship. Large companies in industry after industry are losing clients to their smaller competitors. The fundamental problem with many of these companies is arrogance from past success. That has blinded them to what is occurring in the competitive marketplace. With staff cutbacks and price competition, the larger businesses tend to focus their resources on their big customers to the detriment of smaller ones. This creates an opportunity.

Improving customer service doesn't just come from providing your staff with smile training. Neither does it mean signing service proclamations and making speeches to the staff about how important customers are. Doing is more important than saying. Be a role model, and start with your own people. Be good to them. They're your greatest resource. They're part of your winning team, and everyone's got a job to do.

Customer service must be an organizationwide commitment, from top to bottom, that focuses all of the business's resources toward one goal: delighting customers. Unfortunately, in many businesses, there is a huge chasm between management's professions of commitment to customers and the actual quality of service delivered. What goes wrong? The problem ranges from senior management's failure to communicate to frontline staff and middle managers entrenched in old, familiar patterns. They have lived with poor customer service for so long that they psychopathically fail to see anything wrong with their thinking.

Just like a ball club, there can be addition by subtraction, whereby clubs can strengthen themselves by finding key players with the desire and ability to perform and getting rid of those who don't measure up. This can be true in business as well.

Top management must be explicit to employees about what is expected of them—not just what their job description says, but to do whatever is in their power to satisfy customers. Start a cultural revolution by focusing on the customer. Reeducate your staff.

Now is the time to be sure that your idea of good service and the customers' concept of good service are the same. Service is in the eye of the beholder. Do not assume for a moment that you know what's best for a customer. You may be right, but you must take time to listen. Even if you are the expert, it's a collaborative effort. Really listening to customers must become the rule of business. Remember, you never learn anything from listening to yourself. Good service results when you exceed your customers' expectations.

Exceptional service should be so memorable for customers that it creates lifetime loyalty and many word-of-mouth referrals. The cost of good service? Very little. The payoff? Your annuity—and the satisfaction that you're a quality operation with a special business ethic. The simple requirement for exceptional service is just treating the customer right. Customer service is nothing other than people dealing with people.

Now at this point, you might be saying, "Oh, it's just a variation on the Golden Rule, 'Treat the customer as I'd like to be treated if the roles were reversed.'" There's logic in that, but there's also a trap! Your roles are not reversed. You must treat customers as *they* want to be treated. Customer service is all a matter of perception. What is important to you may not be all that important to your customers, and vice versa. Go beyond yourself. Get into your customers' shoes and try to see things from their perspective. Although you are trying to make a sale, be more of a counselor than purely a salesperson.

At your peril, never take customers for granted. No matter what you may have done for them in the past, it is what you are doing for them now that matters to them.

A satisfied customer receives what is expected. But when a customer receives more than expected, you've got a delighted customer. Delighted customers are many times more profitable to you than merely satisfied customers. While satisfied customers have no complaints, they will listen to offers from your competition. But delighted customers think that your company is the best. And they'll spread positive words about your company, which generates new business.

Aim higher! Aim for the superb level of service, and turn your satisfied customers into delighted customers. Don't just satisfy them, delight them! Show that you genuinely care.

Superb service is not achieved through price reductions. It is achieved through adding value to the service. Added value always comes through people. Product intangibles come through you and your people. And often, it's the little things—the details and the follow-up—that make all the difference.

The mark of a sound business is a loyal customer base. As all successful businesses know, happy customers do much of your selling for you. You will find them promoting your interests within their own organization and outside of it, helping to boost your sales. They know that you are the best, a winner, and in effect want to link themselves to your rising star, to be associated with you.

WHY POOR SERVICE COSTS YOU*

- 96% of all unhappy customers never complain.
- 91% of those who are unhappy do not come back.
- Each unhappy customer will, on average, tell 9 to 10 others.
- You will retain 82% to 95% of unhappy customers if you fix the problem. If you handle the problem well, it can build tremendous customer loyalty.

A market research firm found that 68% of customers made a switch for no particular reason. In other words, their former supplier lost the business because they made no real effort to retain them. They took the customers for granted. How much more prosperous would these firms be today if they had retained those customers?

When businesses differentiate themselves from their competitors with customer-driven service, customers will often pay a premium for their products or services. Market surveys show that about one-third of customers are relatively insensitive to service price.

It is important to keep in mind that the actual sale is just a preliminary proceeding; the sale really starts after the order is placed. That's when the customer finds out whether you can deliver on what you promise. What you do before the sale is not as important as what you do after it. Timely delivery, product satisfaction, and service are what the customer is looking for. A satisfied customer does not have to be resold.

For most companies, improving the quality and character of their customer service is probably their best competitive opportunity.

Successful businesses manage their customers with the same care they put into managing their products. Customers are as important as products. No business can exist without customers.

**Source:* Technical Assistance Research Programs, Washington, D.C.

Those businesses that commit to superb customer service benefit on the bottom line. And you'll also have happier employees who are motivated to put forth their best effort.

SUPERB CUSTOMER SERVICE

Superb customer service means seeing things from the customers' perspective. It means serving customers the way customers would serve themselves if given the opportunity. The customers' definition is the only one that matters.

Therefore, ask your customers what they want. And ask your competitors' customers, too. Find out where you differ. Ask both groups questions such as:

- Why did you choose us/them?
- What do we/they do best?
- What are our/their weakest points?
- How can we/they improve?
- What must we/they do to retain your business?

Employees at all levels of the company, from the CEO and top management on down, need to actively participate in these customer audits. You need to take the time to visit customers. Talk to them one-on-one. Often they will provide new insights into how your product or service is actually used. Such input can be invaluable in a competitive market. You need to understand why they are buying from you and how that may change in the future. Just filling orders is a sure way to fail. It's often best to invite your most innovative customers to recommend new ideas. In these informal discussions, ask them to be completely honest about the product or service that they buy from you or your competitors. Act on what they tell you! Do not treat this as an exercise. Listen, learn, and act. At the same time, your customers will appreciate that you're not standing still, but always striving to improve.

Too many business owners and executives consider customer contact the responsibility of the sales staff. However, the opportunity to gain insights from customers is a vital element in setting goals for the business. Top management should spend a day in the life of key customers—to learn, look, and listen, not to sell.

A survey of customers will usually show that most are happy with your product or service. They must be, or they would not be customers. Just as in the sports world, where you often learn more from defeat than from victory, the criticisms of that small group of dissatisfied customers can provide the most important information. They can identify why others are not customers, why you lose customers, and why potential customers choose your competitors. The negative opinions expressed by the minority can provide the best idea of where your weaknesses are. Former customers can be a goldmine for such information. This can also be an opportunity to reclaim lost customers, who can represent a major source of profits. They thought enough of you to do business with you previously, and perhaps can be induced to do so again.

You may find that few of your competitors bother to perform such an audit. Ask potential customers what you must do to have them buy your product, and you may be surprised when they ask for something very simple and easy to provide. Often just asking will win you their business. It immediately shows a willingness to work with them and meet special requests.

Researchers at the Marketing Science Institute in Cambridge, Massachusetts, found that these were the most important characteristics of service quality as seen by the customer.

- *Reliability:* Doing what was promised—always the most important factor. Customers expect dependable, accurate, and consistent performance. Unkept promises are a major source of dissatisfaction. Keep your promises.
- *Responsiveness:* Also known as promptness and helpfulness.

- *Assurance:* Staff should be knowledgeable and courteous and should convey confidence in the service they provide.
- *Warmth:* Customers like personal attention from a polite individual who listens well.

HOW TO DELIVER SUPERB SERVICE

The desire to provide superb customer service must permeate all thinking within the company, from the top to the lowest levels. The focus of all business activity should be directed toward satisfying customers. Whatever customers want, customers get. Shift the focus from standards set by management to standards set by customers. Customize your service to what I term "customerize." Strive to meet the unique requirements of each and every customer.

The most important change your company will make is a change in attitude. The thought of obtaining the customers' goodwill should pervade the organization and permeate every decision, every procedure, and every step in every department. And the outcome is just an aggregate of all the exchanges with your customers.

Start a customer revolution. Look at every aspect of the operation from the customers' perspective. Many of the changes made will be very small. But, like a series of ripples growing into a wave, collectively they can produce a quantum leap in your level of service. As with quality improvement, there is no finish line in the pursuit of customer service excellence. Every day, your customers must be won over anew.

EMPLOYEE SATISFACTION AND CUSTOMER SATISFACTION GO TOGETHER

Your employees are the key to good customer service. In too many businesses, employees view a customer with a problem as a nuisance. If you want to effect real change, you must first get your people to understand the frustrations your customers experience. Have them role-play as customers and experience what the customers must endure.

Another effective method to get your staff's attention is to videotape customers talking about what they find frustrating in dealing with your company. It's amazing how quickly there is recognition of a problem when the videos are played back to the staff. Your employees must understand that customers are the sole judge of quality, and that all can learn from customers' criticisms or suggestions.

The first rule here is to always treat your employees in the same manner that you want them to treat your customers. There is so much we take for granted. We assume that we are treating our employees well. But are we really? If they have a poor impression of management, or the business as a whole, how well are they going to perform and convey the correct impression to your customers? Therefore, to repeat, the first rule is to take care of your employees. If you take care of them, they will take care of your customers. Your employees are management's customers. Treat them accordingly.

The employees who deal most frequently with the public are often the lower-level people in the company. These people are the ambassadors for your business. Are you treating and training them accordingly? Your frontline people—sales, service, or distribution—can make or break you. They must be trained extensively, not just as a one-time effort, but ongoing. They should participate in the management meetings held to evaluate customer service. If they do not attend, how useful can the meetings be anyway?

When your frontline people are kept well informed and feel a part of the decision-making process, they will feel a special commitment to ensure that the business succeeds. A business with a special commitment to its employees breeds a matching commitment from them. The person closest to the customer creates the greatest impression.

Define for your staff what good service means in your business. Frontline staff need guidelines in making decisions and need to have confidence in how to resolve difficult situations. However, all of these noble thoughts will not be of much value if you do not empower your employees with the authority to deal with a customer's problem and give them the training to do so. Streamline your selling, ordering, and distribution systems to smooth the way for your employees in their efforts to better serve your customers. Give them latitude and responsibility so that they feel they may take the initiative. This can create a positive environment for both the customer and the employee. The payoff can be significant. Sales will rise, as will morale, productivity, and quality. Also, when frontline employees are empowered to solve problems and take better care of customers, there may not be a need for a level of supervisors or middle managers. The more authority is passed on down, the less need there may be for such a management level. It is important to get the decision-making closer to the customers. Flatten your organization chart. Since your employees involved in customer service are closest to your customers, they are a potential goldmine of information. Capitalize on this. Ask them on a regular basis for their input about improvements. This kind of empowerment reduces stress for these employees, and at the same time helps them to be happier and more productive.

To emphasize this point of employee involvement, let me quote from a man who knew what he was talking about: Sam Walton, the founder of Wal-Mart.

> *The more you share profits with your associates—whether it's in salaries or incentives or bonuses or stock discounts—the more profit will accrue to the company. Why? Because the way management treats the associates is exactly how the associates will then treat the customers. And if the associates treat the customers well, the customers will return again*

> *and again, and that is where the real profit in this business lies, not in trying to drag strangers into your stores for one-time purchases based on splashy sales or expensive advertising. Satisfied, loyal, repeat customers are at the heart of Wal-Mart's spectacular profit margins, and those customers are loyal to us because our associates treat them better than salespeople in other stores do. So, in the whole Wal-Mart scheme of things, the most important contact ever made is between the associate in the store and the customer.* [Sam Walton, *Made in America* (New York: Doubleday, 1991)]

CUSTOMER FEEDBACK

Your customers will often be the best source for ideas. Don't guess at what they expect. Invest dollars in getting their feedback. Find out through surveys, questionnaires, phone interviews, and the like exactly what they want. Let them tell you how to serve them even better.

No company can stand still. You must constantly adjust to trends and a changing marketplace. Your company must be dynamic and always reinventing itself. You must be open to new ideas and approaches. Never think that you have all of the answers. Always be willing to experiment with new ideas on how to better serve your customers.

Here are some suggestions on how to do so:

- Suggestion cards/questionnaires: Keep them brief with just a few specific questions to encourage a response.

  —"Would you recommend our product/service to a friend?"

  —"Did you have any problems making the purchase?"

  —"Did you experience any problems with the delivery?"

—"Did you experience any problems using the product?"

Request that they elaborate on their response. Put your fax number on the card or questionnaire, or include a postage-paid envelope.

- Focus groups: Have regular meetings with your customers. Get their direct feedback on items such as price, packaging, quality, delivery, and service. Then take action. Use such groups to get advice on all aspects of your business, from product quality through after-sales service.
- Cold calling: All employees, from the frontline staff to the CEO, should contact a number of customers every week. Doing so will emphasize to all the importance of customers and that they not be taken for granted. This is very important. All too often, staff—including the CEO—get caught up in the daily operational issues and forget that *satisfying customers is the most important issue.*

  During these calls it is important to put aside your own ego. Don't be defensive, otherwise you run the risk of turning off the customer. Sit patiently and listen. Treat a complaint as an opportunity to learn and to satisfy a customer. Thank them, and call back with the results and impact of their input.
- Toll-free numbers: Make it easy for customers to communicate with you, or your competition will do it for you. In some large corporations, senior managers often answer these calls themselves to get direct feedback from their customers.
- Mystery customers: You may wish to pose as a mystery customer yourself, if that is possible, or ask friends or relatives to do so. Find out for yourself what hurdles or bureaucratic nonsense your customers have to contend with.

SOME FINAL THOUGHTS

- You have less to fear from competitors than you do from providing bad service.
- The customers who don't speak up are the ones you have to watch—the silent ones. They say nothing and may take their business elsewhere. Get them talking. Get feedback!
- Bend the rules to please customers. Never say "I can't." Your staff should be able to quickly satisfy a customer's request, even when the request is somewhat beyond the norm.
- Make it easy for a customer to solve a problem. Do not compound matters by making it difficult for them to file a complaint or gain a swift resolution of a problem. Leave filibusters and delays to your competitors. Don't let that be a part of your service.
- Promise only what you can deliver. Do not raise customer expectations to a level that you cannot meet.
- Depending on the nature of your business, it may be beneficial for key members of your staff at various levels to visit your customers' operations. That face-to-face meeting, and the opportunity to see your product from the customers' point of view, can prove extremely helpful.
- Deliver the service that your customers really want. Never mind the unimportant things; how you handle the important services is what count.
- Listen carefully to your customers' suggestions for additional or enhanced services. Never stop asking about their changing needs. If there is a market for them, this could provide a new source of revenue. Most new business comes from existing customers.
- Train the staff not to act defensively when dealing with irate customers, but just to focus on solving the problem. Often

customers will know that the staff person is not responsible, but they just want to vent at somebody in the company who will listen. Recognition and acceptance of customers' problems, together with polite treatment, are very important.

- To help in building a competitive and winning attitude among your staff, assign them the responsibility for keeping tabs on the competition. This provides a source to measure themselves against.
- Maintain a list of "problem customers"—those most likely to jump to a competitor. Make sure that they get special attention.

SUMMARY

In summary, the two keys to a successful customer service program are:

1. Treating your employees as you expect them to treat your customers.
2. Establishing a culture that focuses on meeting customers' needs.

Acquiring new customers can be both time-consuming and expensive, with no guarantee of success. With advertising and promotion costs, you might spend $500 to capture a $100 first order. If you don't keep the customer for some years, you don't make money. A long-term payback is necessary to cover the expense of finding the customer. Developing new products can be expensive and risky, but improving your service level is not—and it can yield significant benefits to your bottom line. Long-term customers have lower sales costs and higher profits. If you do not change or improve your service level, your competition will do it for you.

Customers are too precious a commodity to be taken for granted. They are the lifeblood of your business. Every decision you make must be based on customer desires. Your customers determine whether you are going to succeed or fail. If you do not please them and listen to them, you will not succeed. Your service must be impeccable. Superb customer service is your best weapon in combating employee apathy and promoting customer loyalty. Understand your market, and make every sale result in a satisfied customer. Make sure that customer service is a part of your product, not apart from it.

6 Business Planning

Some people hope. Other people plan.

—Peter Drucker

Business, more than any other occupation, is a continual dealing with the future; it is a continual calculation, an instinctive exercise in foresight.

—Henry K. Luce

Many entrepreneurs and business managers consider planning to be the preserve of paper shufflers. This may be true in large corporations, some of which have planned themselves out of existence, primarily by casting a plan in concrete and then sinking with it.

Entrepreneurs enjoy the thrill of operating a business—the personal challenge involved; pushing themselves all the time. Planning is often the last thing on their minds. When planning, they do not always feel that they are accomplishing anything worthwhile, so they put it off. However, if they do not plan, eventually the odds are that they will pay a heavy price. Risk takers are usually gamblers, not entrepreneurs. The most successful entrepreneurs are those who can figure out how not to incur risks. There is no point in taking a risk that you do not have to take. If you take on enough risk, eventually it will get you.

If you want to achieve significant growth, you need order, not chaos. Things need to be well-planned and well-thought-out. For long-term success, you need radar and a good map. Businesses that do not plan are generally one-man shows. They are usually very limited in what they can achieve. Operating on instinct does not work in the long term. Aiming to be "the biggest and the best" is not a goal; at best it is a wish. A business without a plan is like a ship without a rudder.

For established businesses, a good business plan is an early warning system. Properly completed, it allows you to anticipate potential problems. The business world is dynamic and challenging. Many factors can affect your business such as new technology, new competitors, changes in government regulations, or the local and national economies. If you do not plan, you may not recognize a problem until it is too late. You are in a better position to see early warning signs when you have a plan, and then can take prompt corrective action, or implement contingency plans already in place.

When people think of a business plan they usually think of start-up companies seeking investors. Ongoing businesses should, and usually do, develop business plans. Probably every large business in existence has a detailed short-term and long-term plan.

When you first start a business, you may not need too much of a map. However, as you grow and add staff, you start to delegate authority. At that point, people need to know where the business is headed. When staff complains about autocratic management or indecisiveness at the top—management constantly changing its mind or holding all decision-making authority to itself—they become disenchanted, morale drops, and productivity is affected.

In these situations, the CEO tends to blame the staff, when it is actually he or she who is at fault. Having a sense of where the business is headed is not for the CEO alone to guard that knowledge like private, privileged information, isolating everyone else from it.

It is best to bring everyone into the process and get everyone on the same page of the play book. You might be calling the plays from the bench, so to speak, but everyone needs to know the play in order to execute. Sharing your vision with your employees means making your goals their goals.

Through the planning process, the CEO can communicate the vision for the company and in return get invaluable feedback from staff. The participatory nature of the process can galvanize all. You will find that you have got more motivated employees who are not only working *for* you, but *with* you. That is an important distinction.

Now you are nearly convinced of the need for planning, but would like some reinforcement before taking the plunge. "How will it really increase my profits?" you may be asking. Peter Drucker perhaps answered that question best when he wrote that what gets planned, gets done. The development of a sound, realistic plan to grow your sales and profits stands you a much better chance of achievement than if you had no such plan. Businesses need well-thought plans if they are to become the leaders in the marketplace rather than the followers or the vanquished.

A plan also offers the following benefits:

- It helps to focus your activities by organizing your thoughts and developing a specific group of long-term objectives.
- A full analysis of all factors affecting the business—that is, the market, the product, management, and finances—is necessary to the well-being of a business, and the planning process requires that you undertake that analysis.
- It is a goal-oriented guide that maps out where you are going and how you are going to get there, including alternate routes if the main way is blocked.
- It permits you to make mistakes on paper rather than in the real world.

- Involvement of key staff members in the planning process helps develop a sense of vested interest and pride that can prove invaluable.
- Should you need to raise additional capital or borrowings, most lenders or investors will not put money into a business without first reviewing the business plan.
- It replaces the separate, and perhaps disjointed, marketing, financial, and operational plans with one comprehensive plan.
- It creates benchmarks by which progress can be measured.

In summary, a business plan is an excellent vehicle for planning both the short-term and long-term operations of a business and for moving a business beyond its current level to another level of growth.

WHAT IS A BUSINESS PLAN?

A business plan is a written document, usually covering a one- to five-year time span, that is a statement of business objectives together with the strategies describing how the objectives will be met.

HOW TO PROCEED

It is important to understand first that real planning takes guts. You have to be willing to ask questions that you may never have asked previously. You need to consider all aspects of the business, both good and bad, or you will be wasting your time. Planning goes beyond wishful thinking to considering what it will actually take, step by step, to achieve your objectives.

The goal is to produce a focused, realistic plan that has the support of all staff members that are necessary for its successful implementation. Accepting the fact that no one individual possesses all of the wisdom and vision necessary to develop a successful plan is important. Rather, it is vitally important that all of the human resources available contribute to the process to ensure that the objectives developed are sound, accepted, supported, and acted on. This two-way process enables you to communicate your vision for the business, and in return receive the feedback from your staff. Small businesses in particular need this dialogue, as many of their owners tend to be autocratic. You cannot exist in a vacuum, make good decisions, or develop good plans unless you are inviting and receiving good input from your associates. If your door is closed, so is your mind.

Once this is agreed on, then it is time to move forward. Gather together the key people from all areas of the business, for example, manufacturing, operations, marketing, sales, finance, distribution, and so on. Planning is most successful when it is a participatory process; thus, it is important that all facets of the business are represented. This free-to-speak corporate powwow will reveal the business's strengths, weaknesses, opportunities, and threats for examination from different aspects and viewpoints. Out of such a meeting or series of meetings should come an orchestrated plan that all departments feel a part of and can sign on to.

Creativity and brainstorming can be the keys to such sessions, and all should be encouraged to participate and make suggestions. The leader of the session should facilitate an open forum that can elicit the best from everyone. The CEO should approach the session with a totally open mind and strongly encourage all to speak their minds openly.

It is important that all of those present contribute, not just the more verbose or forthcoming staff members. Candor is obviously terribly important, as the worst thing that can happen is to have individuals present who fear to tread on the turf of their colleagues or function merely as sycophants. Correctly designed probes can help to overcome this problem and bring about full and candid participation.

The hardest part of planning is getting started. All participants should be asked to identify what they see as the business's strengths, weaknesses, opportunities, and threats. Defining what the business's strengths are is very important, then seek to build on them. Continue the proceedings by asking questions such as the following:

- What business are we in? What is our market? Is it growing, dying, or standing still?
- What is our place in the industry? How can we improve on that? What market segment opportunities are there? What does our sales trend tell us? Are we innovative in responding to the market? What are the key factors for growth?
- Who is our competition? What can we learn from them? In what areas are they better than us? Why don't their customers buy from us?
- How effective is our marketing? What is our market share? What share of the market do we want now? Next year? Five years from now? What is the return on our marketing budget? Is our advertising effective?
- What is our corporate image? What is our image to our customers? Who are our customers? Who are our potential customers? How happy are they with our product? Our service? Why do they buy from us? Do they recommend us to others? Do they want change in our product? Or a brand-new product?
- What are the trends in our industry? Are we prepared? What contingencies should we make? Is forthcoming government legislation going to affect us?
- How do our products or services compare with the competition? How can we improve our products or services? What new products or services should we be offering?

- How can we improve our operations? Our productivity? Can new technology or improved work methods help? What are the staff's suggestions?
- What are our personnel needs? What is the job satisfaction level of our employees? How can we improve it? How does our employee turnover rate compare with the industry and area? How can we better train our staff? How do employees view our personnel policies? How can we improve their attendance level?
- How can we make our jobs easier or more efficient? What redundant reports do we produce? What time-wasting activities can be eliminated?
- What is our greatest strength? How well do we use it?
- What is our greatest weakness? How can we rectify it?
- How can we further improve our quality level? How can we improve supplier relationships?
- How do we increase revenues? Does our pricing strategy need rethinking? Are our prices competitive? Where in the market are we pricing our products/services?
- How do we reduce expenditures? Should we set an arbitrary goal and work toward it? Why not?
- How can we finance growth? How do we improve our cash flow? What are our goals to achieve fiscal stability/profit improvement?
- Where do we want to be five years from now? What steps do we need to take now and in the future to achieve that objective?
- How can we strive for excellence in all that we do?

Your goals should be:

- Clear, in writing, with a specific time frame.

- Challenging. Small steps inspire and challenge no one. They capture no imaginations. Seemingly impossible goals are exciting, bringing out the best in people.
- Measurable, so that they can be monitored and compared with the actual results.
- Flexible, so that the targets may be altered as situations change.

Every business, large or small, will succeed or fail based on a few key strategic factors or overriding goals, not a dozen or two. This is a very important point. The group should seek to ascertain those key factors that will be responsible for future success, then pursue them. Pursuing a host of factors will usually mean that none of them are fully achieved. Focus on those two or three key strategic factors that will be instrumental in achieving future success.

Adequate financing is usually one such key factor. Other factors can be just as important.

Once the key strategic factors have been established, the next step is to identify strategic objectives for the implementation of each factor. As with all objectives, it is important that they be quantifiable.

Example:

Key strategic factor: Increase sales.

Strategy objective:

- Aggressive marketing to expand customer base by 20%.
- Expand sales to existing customers by 10%.
- Open new stores to produce a cash/credit card sales increase of 15%.

  $ . . . sales by 12/31/19x1

  $ . . . sales by 12/31/19x2

  $ . . . sales by 12/31/19x3

  $ . . . sales by 12/31/19x4

  $ . . . sales by 12/31/19x5

Key strategic factor: Improve cash flow.

Strategy objective:

- Reduce average accounts receivable to 35 days.
- Reduce inventory to 42 days.
- Expand holding period on accounts payable to 35 days.

Key strategic factor: Become more competitive.

Strategy objective:

- A 3% reduction in direct wage cost per unit through productivity gains.
- A 4% reduction in suppliers' per-unit costs.
- A 5% price reduction to match competitors.

Within each strategy objective, depending on its nature, further detailing of the steps necessary for its implementation may be necessary. These steps are usually known as tactical objectives.

Example:

Strategy objective: Reduce accounts receivable to 35 days.

Tactical objective:

- Invoice for goods within 24 hours of shipping.
- Advise all customers of credit terms.
- Perform credit check on all new customers.
- Hire a full-time collection person.

Once objectives have been established, it is of the utmost importance that responsibility for their implementation be assigned to specific individuals and realistic target dates be set.

The objectives developed will impact revenue, expense, and cash flow to various extents, and these factors need to be reflected in your financial plan. The plan needs to consider the potential impact of each objective on these factors, so that they may be prioritized and reflected in future budgets. Depending on the business's cash availability, delaying certain objectives may be necessary until the financing is in place to provide for them.

Restraining one's enthusiasm in setting target dates for each objective is important. Recognizing that each individual already has a full load of work to handle, sufficient time must be allotted to achieve the specific objectives assigned. Otherwise, the plan cannot be implemented effectively.

FOLLOW-THROUGH

Do not prepare a business plan, review it, then consign it to a drawer. Businesses should see the plan as a living document. To achieve the most effective results, the CEO should be responsible for monitoring the plan. It is the CEO's responsibility to make certain that all objectives are being met as prescribed. This follow-up should be done at least quarterly. Backsliding should not be allowed.

Very few plans are ever executed exactly as written. This happens in part because the plans are poorly developed, but also because the marketplace is constantly changing: Customer preferences change, a project takes longer than expected, or a key competitor introduces a new product or service. Management needs to have the flexibility to respond to these new or unexpected conditions, either with contingent actions provided by the plan or new courses of action.

Many businesses update their plans annually. However, sometimes that is too long a time frame, and more frequent updates such as quarterly or semiannually may be preferable. A plan that is not updated throughout the year may be worth little with the passage of time. Remember that forecasting is usually very difficult, especially when it concerns the future!

WHY BUSINESS PLANS FAIL

There is often a corporate culture, a set way of doing things, that can lead to resistance to change. This is where leadership must be shown and follow-through implemented.

The other principal reasons for failure are:

- Incorrectly defined strategies, or a misperception of the marketplace.
- Objectives that are not stated in quantifiable terms.
- Objectives lacking detailed implementation plans delineating the various tasks and responsibilities.
- Plans that are not updated as needed.
- The input and support of important staff members were either not received or not acted on during the development process.

Do not set the plan up for failure by setting too-ambitious goals. Lower your sights perhaps a little, and as the plan moves forward and confidence grows, push the goals higher.

FUTURE PERIODS

The ongoing updating of the business plan allows it to address more current conditions and serve as a benchmark to measure actual performance. The previous year's plan can tell you whether a particular strategy was effective or ineffective, and what implementation strategies worked most effectively. Comparing actual performance with the plan helps identify strengths and weaknesses in the company that can be acted on.

All of this is useful and important in preparing future years' plans. The strategies outlined for the future will have a basis in past strategies, taking into account what worked and what didn't. Overall, it makes the preparation of future years' plans easier and provides for greater accuracy and effectiveness.

SUMMARY

Generally, planners outperform nonplanners. The reason is that formal plans are better than informal plans, since the process of developing the plan forces the consideration of many ideas, issues, and objectives. The more detailed the planning processes, the better the business's opportunity for performance.

7 Good Management Makes the Difference

In venture capital, the experts say that management is the most important single factor, and that no matter what business a company is in, bad management will wreck it and good management will save it.

—A. David Silver, *The Inside Raider*

Burdened with the day-to-day affairs of business or a simple lack of knowledge, many owners and executives of small and medium-size companies are just flying by the seat of their pants when trying to manage their business. A sense of direction, knowing their true costs of doing business, marketing—these are all areas that are either vague or very much wanting.

Some companies enjoy initial success through luck or by being in the right place at the right time. Their product or service might have been new or unique, or maybe there was not much competition with which to contend. Some, foolishly, assume that their success was due to their innate ability.

Perhaps sophisticated business skills were not essential to the company's launch. Hanging out the shingle was enough. Still, as a business grows or an industry or geographical area matures, the requisite management skills are essential if a company is to succeed and prosper.

The previous chapters have presented many skills, approaches, and mind-sets for successful business management. In this final chapter, we will cover other essentials. If management concentrates on the business fundamentals and constantly follows up, there is no reason that the business should not achieve greater profits year after year.

THE "INTANGIBLE" BALANCE SHEET

Understanding a balance sheet is of utmost importance. You must not only understand what it tells you, but also what it cannot tell you.

As you probably know, your balance sheet tells how much cash you have in the bank; your receivables, or how much you are owed by your customers; and the value of your inventory, property, and equipment. On the liability side, it tells you how much you owe and how much equity there is in the business.

With a business, you must go beyond the numbers and interpretive schema of the balance sheet. You must have an understanding of what might be termed your "intangible" corporate assets:

- Market share/position
- Product portfolio
- Product quality
- Distribution system
- Your people
- Customer base
- The equity in your name

These intangible corporate assets—when properly understood, managed, and cared for—are probably worth more to your business than the assets that appear on your balance sheet. To a large extent, they are the body of your company, and your balance sheet is the shadow or reflection of that body of assets. These "intangible" assets are the major aggregate of factors behind the numbers.

Should you receive an offer to sell the business, you can be sure that the prospective purchaser will have evaluated these "intangible" assets very carefully. Inventory, receivables, and equipment are very important, but your prospective purchaser will want to know all about your underlying "intangible" assets because they will generate the future revenue and profits.

If your prospective purchaser would be concerned with these "intangible" assets, shouldn't you be? Doesn't it make sense to preserve and develop these assets? Of course it does!

The proper conservation and development of these "intangible" assets requires an investment of time, money, patience, and the long-term view. The investment must be continuous and ongoing. Assuredly, such an investment will yield a very important payoff—a company with a good name, quality products, satisfied and delighted customers, efficiency and lower operating costs or repeat business, and a positive corporate culture with motivated, congenial "partners" in your enterprise.

Your investment in these "intangible" assets will pay off like an annuity year after year, increasing in value. It will probably be the one investment you make that will give you your greatest return. You can liken these ideas to a foundation. The stronger it is, the more your company can withstand the vicissitudes of the marketplace and prosper.

Your accounting system, and the reports that it produces, do not measure your "intangible" assets. By their nature, save for market share and position, these assets cannot be quantified. Since businesses rely on their financial reports to determine how they are doing, they look to their operating profit and make the assumption that if profits are healthy and increasing, all must be well. However, it is a leap of faith to conclude that this success will continue. A business may have been liquidating its "intangible" assets in order to achieve a short-term profit. That liquidation will not be immediately apparent on the financial report. However, if you keep chipping away at your foundation, there is bound to be a collapse or a costly repair.

Many businesses that have shown good profits for a period of time may have done so only because they were not incurring the expense of preserving and developing their "intangible" assets. On the other hand, a business with a poor profit history may be about to produce improved results or even a dramatic turnaround, because it has been investing in its "intangible" assets. One thing is for certain: When you do not invest in the future, there is not a future—or at least, not a very good one.

By all accounts, regaining one's competitive position is a lot more expensive than maintaining the current position. It has been estimated that it costs five times as much to recruit a new customer as it costs to retain an existing one. If quality drops, how do you ever persuade a lost customer to return? If your company loses staff due to an autocratic management style and word spreads, it becomes that much more difficult to attract and retain qualified people.

To summarize, not caring for your "intangible" assets brings no lasting benefit. One must think long term when it comes to operating and managing a business. The least successful businesses are the "treasure hunters." These are the companies that pursue a short-term strategy, satisfied to gain a quick financial result at the expense of making the investment for the long term. If you want your business to grow and prosper and to pay you a healthy return while increasing in value, make the investment now. You will be thankful that you did. Watch your balance sheet; however, care for, preserve, and develop your "intangible" assets, for they represent the real wealth of your business. The future success of your business depends on them.

HOW BUSINESSES PROSPER

Why do some businesses grow and prosper while others struggle and fail? There is much to be learned from both paths: what to do and what not to do.

First, let us look at successful businesses. In addition to the points detailed elsewhere in this book, what do successful businesses do or have in common?

You may find it useful to refer to an article entitled, "Managing for Tomorrow," coauthored by Robert Buzzell of Harvard University and Mark J. Chussil of the Strategic Planning Institute (*Sloan Management Review*, summer 1985). Based on their study of nearly 200 businesses over an eight-year period, Buzzell and Chussil found that management often pursues a nearsighted strategy of short-term profitability at the expense of long-term competitive strength. For the long-term success of a business, this approach must be reversed.

The authors found that many businesses have the potential to do much better than they have done, with management often emphasizing cash flow to the detriment of building greater long-term value.

How do we rectify this and improve the value of the business? The businesses in the study that performed the best were in strong market positions and were competing in growing markets. Good performance was strongly associated with aggressive marketing and investment support. Good performance, therefore, resulted from an aggressive strategy supported by adequate spending.

> *[The authors] observed sharp contrasts between good, average, and poor performers. Good performers increased their marketing outlays at rates much faster than those at which their markets grew. The same pattern held true for each of the two primary components of marketing budgets, sales force and*

> *advertising and promotion. Average performers marketing outlays outpaced their market's growth by smaller margins than the winners, while poor performers' spending levels tended to lag behind their markets.*

In addition, they invested more in new plant capacity, further adding to their long-term value.

The authors caution,

> *The fact that most of the successful businesses expanded their sales force budgets while gaining market shares does not necessarily mean that increased selling activity alone created the share gains. Most likely, businesses captured market shares via a combination of spending more, improving quality, introducing new products, and other competitive actions.*

All of this "does not, of course, mean that managers can buy good performance simply by throwing money at businesses, especially those with relatively weak competitive positions."

Marketing expenditures should be maintained in good times and bad. They should be considered in the same vein as capital outlays: investments that drive revenue over time. Never cut marketing dollars when times are bad. Do not give up the market position you have earned. Your sales force is one of your most important assets. It takes a long time to find and develop good salespeople who know how to sell and produce a profit. Don't disillusion them by cutting back when the economy is off; you need them as much then as when the economy is good.

For long-term success, therefore, you need to make the investment now and plough the profits back into the business to reap the greatest rewards.

"WHAT WENT WRONG?"

On a less happy note, what can you learn from businesses that have run into problems or have not been successful? What signs of future business problems should you be on the lookout for? The first sign is usually the most difficult of all to spot, because it relates to none other than yourself. In the same manner that success starts at the top, so do all problems start at the top. Yes, one person—if that person is the CEO—can make the difference. While management as a whole has an important role to play, there is little doubt that the quality of the person at the top is crucial. Among the causes of business failure, the most significant is undoubtedly the quality, or lack thereof, of the CEO. One-man rule (a.k.a. "big ego") or autocratic rule is the most frequent reason why businesses have failed or are in serious trouble. An autocrat or egomaniac at the top spells trouble. Many CEOs view their business as an extension of themselves, an extension of their ego. When ego gets in the way, the result is a failure to spot problems.

Entrepreneurs are micromanagers by nature and typically very controlling. Many are not able to make the transition to managing a bigger company. They don't know how to manage when they can't personally track everything that is happening.

If this symptom is found so frequently among businesses in trouble or those that have failed, what must its preponderance be in businesses that are still healthy and producing a profit? It is more prevalent than you might suspect, because doing well is not proof that a corporate dictatorship does not exist. In these cases, a business must try to succeed in spite of it. One-man rule does not just apply to the CEO. It can pertain to any person in a management position who provides autocratic rule. Few managers on any level consider themselves guilty of autocratic rule, when in reality most are. It should certainly be worth a little soul-searching and reflection.

Abraham Lincoln once observed, "Nearly all men can stand adversity, but if you want to test a man's character, give him power."

One-man rule is another name for ineffective leadership. When this problem is present, you will usually find:

- Low morale
- A lack of communication
- Rapid turnover of quality staff
- Deficient supervision
- Failure or fear of individuals to take responsibility or to make decisions
- A loss of focus for the business as it meanders on, ignoring problems that should be addressed

In every business, the CEO and all those in positions of responsibility should become coaches, cheerleaders, or mentors. As Lee Iacocca has said, his job as chairman of Chrysler was to "delegate and motivate." No one person knows all of the answers; nobody is always right. It is very important to encourage and pay attention to the staff's ideas and develop a team spirit; everyone must feel that they are significant and that they have a vested interest, otherwise creativity is stifled. In such an environment, employees can become highly committed. The example is set at the top; all follow your lead. Set the right example to succeed, and you will. It takes a united effort, with everyone committed and doing their best job possible, for the enterprise to succeed fully.

James T. Bere, chairman of the Borg-Warner Corporation, said it best:

> *The job of the top executive is not to make decisions . . . it is to put good people in place and judge if they are making good decisions. You give them the power. When they come in and say, "How do I do something?" I say, "That is your problem."*

Complacency

After autocratic rule, probably the greatest impediment to continuing business success is complacency—being "fat and happy." Everything is going well: Sales are good, profits are up, and the pressure is off. Wrong—once you get on top, others are waiting to knock you down. Something in human nature leads people to rest when they reach the top. However, the only way to go from there is down. Put your victory behind you, otherwise it will be your last. You can never, ever rest on your laurels. Your competitors are not resting on their laurels. They are hungry for your business as they further innovate and pursue your customers. The history of business is replete with tales of businesses that thought they had it made without making an innovative effort to further improve their products or services. Slowly the slippage starts to show, and then it starts to accelerate, for complacency breeds mediocrity. "What is going wrong?" Somebody else will ask, "Why are they [customers] doing this to us?" Customers forget quickly, and rather than saying "Thank you," are more apt to say "What have you done for me lately?"

The marketplace is dynamic and ever-changing. Keep pace with it, or it will run you over. Adapting to changing conditions is difficult. Quite possibly the leaders in your industry five or 10 years ago are different from those in the lead today. Just ask IBM, Sears, or General Motors. There is no place for complacency—be a little paranoid at all times, for your competitors really are out to get you. A new competitor will have no bad habits or ingrained culture to overcome. This absence of history, and the imperative of survival, forces new businesses to be keenly tuned to the needs of the marketplace.

We have dealt with perhaps the most serious impediments to business success and profitability. What are the other signs? They are discussed in the following sections.

Liquidity Crisis

Often the first real sign that a serious problem exists occurs when a liquidity crisis arises. This situation can arise in a number of ways:

- Through undercapitalization. Being thinly capitalized and relying on borrowings to grow places the business in jeopardy.
- Expanding too rapidly. One of the greatest dangers that often confronts a business is too much success. Rapid growth, when led by a bold entrepreneur and supported by large borrowing, can often be a prescription for trouble. Growth must be managed to prevent problems. Working capital must grow along with sales, or cash flow problems will result.
- The business is actually losing money. In these situations, you will usually find some or all of the following:
    1. Management devoting more time responding to calls from vendors.
    2. The business is "playing the float" with the bank—in other words, releasing checks today in anticipation of future deposits.
    3. Sales forecasts are continually optimistic.
    4. Increasing accounts receivable.
    5. Increasing accounts payable.
    6. Falling profit margins.
    7. Inventory turnover is slowing.
    8. Large bad debt writeoffs.
    9. Unit sales volume declining.

Overall, the financial position of the business deteriorates, and will continue to do so, until corrective action is taken. Management must pay extremely close attention to its cash flow projections and constantly update them, because when you are out of cash, you are out of business.

Overdiversification

When an established business enters a new area, it faces the same challenges a new business faces:

- New problems
- New considerations and rules of the game
- New markets

Unless the diversification is correctly managed, tumult can be a common result, as management is often presented with more challenges than it can handle, finding itself frequently overworked and putting out fires. Many entrepreneurs, having achieved success, think that they have the "golden touch" and that any business they pursue will be successful. This is not always the case in the highly specialized world of business that we live in today. Being successful in more than one business at a time is difficult, as a business needs lots of attention.

Diversification efforts take time, resources, and investment that many businesses cannot afford. For many businesses, it is often more sensible to focus on what they do best. If they definitely want to pursue a new area of business besides their existing business, it should be separately established with its own staffing and resources. It should not be allowed to draw from or hurt your present operation.

Corporate history finds many companies that overdiversified retreating to their core business. It was the core business that primarily suffered during the overdiversification period.

Limited Customer Base

A steady, dependable customer is an asset to any business. However, when that customer represents a significant portion of the business revenue, that customer occupies a position of considerable influence.

A limited customer base should be a warning for any business. Should that customer choose to diversify its suppliers or to take all of its business elsewhere, the future of the business can be seriously jeopardized. If this problem pertains to your business, you need to expand your customer base quickly to decrease your financial exposure. A broad customer base is essential for stability.

Lack of Financial Controls

Every business must have:

- Budgets
- Cash flow projections
- Costing systems
- Timely, accurate, and pertinent financial statements

Businesses large and small need sophisticated accounting methods and procedures. They must be aware of their direct labor cost, production costs, profit margins by product line, by division, and other such information necessary to understand and manage their affairs. Old-fashioned bookkeeping is not good enough anymore. You do not need the totals in order to manage, but the detail.

In my experience as a business advisor, smaller businesses get into difficulty more frequently due to financial problems than any other reason, either through overtrading with the amount of capital available, or having inadequate financial records. You *absolutely must* have current, relevant, financial data—by division, product/service line, and so on—on a timely basis. If you are to learn only one thing from this book, this should be it. I have seen too many businesses fail or flounder when they need not have done so if the necessary financial data had been available.

As noted later in this chapter, every business must have a top-quality chief financial officer. A number cruncher is not your answer; a CFO who can read and interpret the numbers is very, very important. A really good financial person can be of immense value to any business.

Just as reading an X-ray or interpreting other diagnostic data is an art, have all of your top people, including your outside advisors, interpret the financial details.

The Peter Principle

Lawrence Peter, in stating his principle, said, "In a hierarchy, every employee tends to rise to his level of incompetence." All too often we see instances of well-meaning individuals promoted into positions of greater authority for which they are not prepared. Commendable as it is to promote from within, there are times when it is best for all involved that fresh people with fresh perspectives be brought in from the outside. A business that only promotes from within eventually becomes inbred, leading to a kind of corporate insularity.

As a business grows, those individuals who were possibly among its first employees move up into positions of greater authority. Or perhaps their position stays the same, but the business has greatly expanded. Either way, in these situations they find themselves in a position possibly more demanding than their talents can handle. Rather than terminating them, an option is to have them occupy the second-level position in their department, with fresh blood brought in to occupy the top spot.

The Changing Marketplace

With the ever-faster pace of change in the world today, principally due to technology, automation, and global competition, there is no such thing as a stable marketplace. Nearly every business is forced to adapt to change, or perish. Warning signs include the following:

- No sense of urgency (also known as "fat and happy")
- An obsolete product
- Loss of market share, or participation in a shrinking industry

- Declining sales
- Customers deserting to competitors

To prevent these problems, you need to get out into the marketplace and see what is selling. This is especially important for the CEO, who must personally see what is occurring. Do not leave it to others or simply rely on reports.

Profits

Your profits are down, and have in fact been declining for some time. What is happening to your business, or to your industry, to cause this? Are your competitors doing better? Have you taken on more overhead in anticipation of expansion, and the expected revenue is not being realized as fast as you had thought? Have your expenses grown out of proportion to the increase in revenues? Are you losing sales to competitors?

Profits can turn into losses rather quickly. What can you do now to prevent this from occurring?

Market Share

On a per-unit basis, are you losing market share? If so, why? What positive steps can you take now that will have a high probability of success? Or, if your industry is shrinking, what is the best course of action?

In Summary

It is believed that, at any point in time, one in five businesses is at risk. Once any of the warning signs are there, there is nothing to be gained from delaying action or engaging in unrealistic thinking. Invariably, things will not improve of their own accord; they will only get worse. Do not delay. Accept that there is a problem, and set about correcting it. When you accept that there is a problem, you are more than halfway toward resolving it.

MANAGEMENT INFORMATION SYSTEMS TO MONITOR KEY INDICATORS

Proper controls provide an early warning system to spot problems in their early stages. Effective controls on the expenses and operation of the business, in addition to relevant and concise reporting of financial and production matters, are very important. Specialists in turning around troubled businesses will often tell you that establishing a control and reporting system is usually the first step in effecting a turnaround. If you do not know the current state of the business, how can you possibly effect a turnaround or manage it? Therefore, if establishing a control and reporting system is necessary to save a business, why not make it a standard operating procedure right at the beginning? A control and reporting system belongs in your company, serving as a steadfast sentinel to protect your corporate health and security.

In addition to such a system, every business must have a top-quality CFO. It is worth spending the extra money to attract the best person. A good CFO can make a significant difference in operating a business, and will usually pay for himself or herself many times over.

Do not assume that just because a person has an accounting degree or qualification, they are suited to serve as a CFO. Unfortunately, too many accountants cannot see the forest for the trees as they get lost in the minutiae of their work. The work of a CFO goes beyond mere number crunching. The CFO needs to be able to read the big picture and link the business's fiscal performance with its objectives and to spot aberrant trends, to be able to identify and focus on what is driving the numbers.

What key indicators should you monitor weekly to stay in control? The following should be part of any CEO's list.

Cash on Hand

A drop in your cash balance can be a sign of a potential problem, whether it is due to an increase in receivables or inventory, poor sales performance, or the business is actually losing money. At the first sign of difficulty here, you should immediately seek to identify the source of the problem and rectify it. Do not allow yourself to run out of cash, or you may have a bigger problem.

Receivables

Watch any aberrant trend in your average days of sales outstanding (DSO) figure. Too great an investment in receivables could be accompanied by a liquidity problem and an increase in bad debts. Review the full receivables detail at least twice monthly.

Inventory

Monitor the average number of days on hand by product line. Keep inventory moving to prevent obsolete stock from accumulating.

Sales

Compare your sales for the most recent week and fiscal year to date with the previous year's figures. An increase in sales means that you may need to increase your accumulation of inventory, and conversely, a drop in sales may signal a need to cut back in inventory. A reduction in sales may also suggest that you need to take a close look at the company's sales efforts or reevaluate your products, service, pricing, positioning, and what new activities your competition might be up to.

Expenses

Compare your expense detail for the most recent period and fiscal year to date with your annual financial plan. Fluctuations should be fully accounted for. Beware of expenses continuing to rise after sales increases have tapered off.

Payroll

No matter what your type of business, this is a crucial number to track. You should be provided as much detail as possible, not just a set of totals. The data should be presented in a format that summarizes for you the costs and time per type of activity, and draws a comparison between it and the matching revenue. You want to increase or at least maintain your level of efficiency and productivity.

Gross Profit Ratios

Monitor the gross profit for the principal products weekly, and for all items monthly. When a ratio is off, dig deeper to find and correct the problem.

Operating Profit

This is usually the first figure examined. Rather than just the amount of the profit, you need to carefully monitor its percentage by product line to net sales and how it compares with industry standards. Any deviation from the financial plan or industry norm should be identified and corrected.

Marketing Results

Tally the number of inquiries received as one way to assess how successful your company is in promoting, advertising, and selling. A drop-off in the number of inquiries can portend a drop-off in sales. Compare the number of inquiries received to the number of sales made to measure your effectiveness at converting them into sales. A decline in your conversion ratio may mean that your promotional efforts are directed at the wrong market, or that your sales staffs are not closing on enough prospects. A decline in inquiries might also mean there are some prevailing market conditions that you must respond to, or that you are overqualifying your sales leads and perhaps losing some.

Sales Volume

Your volume by product line should be accumulated and maintained on a continuous basis. This data can tell you which products are in demand and which may require more marketing effort. It may also signal that a product's life cycle is coming to an end or that a product needs revision, revamping, reformulation, or repositioning in the marketplace. This is a very key area, as volume translates into sales revenue.

Turnaround Time

As purchase orders are received, there is no better way to antagonize customers and lose their goodwill than to delay in filling their order. As time is money and timing is everything, poor turnaround time could be costing your customers big time. Leave them cooling their heels too long, and they will just take a walk! Also, as production cost is directly related to the length of turnaround time, costs can rise and profitable sales can turn into losses. Whether you are in a manufacturing or service business, a problem in this area is usually one of managing the production area, your own suppliers, or the people fulfilling the contract.

Revenue and Profit per Employee

This is a very important ratio, and an excellent means to measure your productivity. For example, if your company has 100 employees and $10 million in annual sales, you are producing $100,000 of sales per employee. In this example, if your operating profit was $1 million, your profit per employee would be $10,000. The key to interpreting the data is to know where you stand compared with your competitors. In this regard, your trade association or Robert Morris and Associates in Philadelphia, who specialize in accumulating such information, may have data available. Were your main competitor achieving $150,000 in sales per employee, they would have a huge productivity and cost advantage over you. You need to have a goal that your numbers are, say, 25% higher on a consistent basis than your competitors. Increased productivity produces lower costs, greater profits, and a tremendous competitive advantage. Now is the time to pursue that productivity growth!

You may wish to add to this list of key control factors any factors that are particularly unique or helpful in managing for your particular industry.

INNOVATE, NOT IMITATE

Change in the business world is a constant. Innovation is the only way to survive. Whereas many innovations fail, firms that do not innovate die. New ideas are vital to a business. There is always a better way to do things and different approaches to every situation. Businesses that remain stationary are like ducks sitting on a pond about to be blown out of the water. Don't be that kind of target for your rivals. Staying on top means scrambling continually for new products, services, equipment, and technology approaches, and accepting some failures. Even the year's Super Bowl winner probably took a few losses during their championship season. Failure is a part of success. As long as it is not an addictive habit, failure is a great teacher if a company can learn from it.

All worthwhile activities have an element of risk. When you drill for oil, you never know if you are actually going to make a strike. Business is no different. The best businesses are those whose managements feel the need to keep moving, developing new and improved products, lowering costs, and improving service. Competition is dynamic; thus, well-run businesses are always running a little scared. Management must create a culture/passion that makes innovation a way of life for everyone. You need to develop a higher level of innovative and creative thinking from your people. They must feel deeply involved in their work and enjoy it to be their most creative. This means increasing freedom and removing barriers, such as the fear of expressing original ideas that threaten the status quo; changing the military-style chain of command that makes staff afraid of making mistakes and losing their jobs or outshining their immediate boss, which creates a threat, tension, and real fear of reprisal. Negative attitudes or indifference toward new ideas must be replaced by open-mindedness and support.

Frequent experimentation encourages the idea that innovation and creative thinking are welcomed, and helps to overcome these obstacles.

Management must realize that it does not possess all of the wisdom or bright ideas, and that bold innovation does not only come from highly educated engineers or "higher ups." Often the apparently small incremental changes that various employees suggest result in long-term improvement. Therefore, all employees must feel empowered to come forward with their suggestions for improvement and innovation. The effective ideas should be implemented, and the originators recognized and rewarded.

Many businesses fail at new product development by trying only to score home runs. If the home run happens, great! Nevertheless, business can realistically pursue incremental innovation, or a continuous improvement strategy. Also working with your customers, you can develop a series of enhancements to your existing products—lighter weight, faster performance, and so on—that can expand their usefulness and desirability.

In summary, the innovative business is willing to learn new ways of doing things and is willing to be flexible, for it understands that ideas ultimately separate the winners from the losers. The innovative business creates a climate conducive to creativity and effectively manages creative individuals. Innovative management emphasizes:

- A commitment to innovate from the top down
- Openness to new ideas
- Employee diversity; employees as partners
- A reward system that encourages employee innovation

CONCLUSION

Too many businesses go on making the same mistakes month after month and year after year. They never sit back, do some soul searching, and ask themselves what fundamental or strategic change they need to make in their thinking or operation. In effect, they perpetuate their problems by not making the hard decisions to make a clean break from the past or to make a fundamental change.

Competitors are always improving and striving to take your business away. To survive and succeed in our competitive world, it helps to recognize you are in an economic battle. The stakes are survival and a company's mission to fulfill its potential. It helps to be a bit paranoid, thinking your competitors are trying to take something from you, but they are! There can be no complacency. A business must—absolutely must—continually strive to improve all aspects of its operation if it is to grow and multiply its profits. And do not forget those "intangible" assets.

Appendix: Profit Patrol

Give your business a profit checkup using the following set of questions. It will be worth the investment of your time.

It is important that you be honest with yourself when completing this checkup. Be introspective, and consider whether every yes answer is as solid as it could be. Any no answer denotes an area requiring attention and follow-up action.

	Yes	No
People		
• We hire only talented and motivated individuals with a history of success and who display good judgment and common sense, people with a vision for what they want to achieve.		
• In hiring we always apply the ACE test (attitude, character, enthusiasm).		
• Our corporate culture allows people to grow and exercise their initiative, and we go past rank and regard all of our employees as partners or associates. They in turn act with the commitment of an owner.		
• We have ongoing incentive and recognition programs. We make a point of showing our people the recognition and appreciation they deserve, and we compensate well, including offering a profit-sharing plan.		

	Yes	No
People *(con't.)*		
• We provide sufficient ongoing training opportunities for people to further develop their skills.		
• Staff turnover is low at all levels.		
• Our goals and priorities are clearly formulated and communicated so everyone can sign on.		
• I give people decision-making power by sufficiently empowering them with the authority to fulfill their responsibilities.		
• I actively solicit my staff's ideas, suggestions, and observations.		
• I give the credit for the success of the business to my people, for it is they who achieved it.		
• My staff are continually encouraged to challenge historical rationales, and I try to remove any fear of speaking up or bucking the status quo.		
• I recognize that the more I expect from my people, the more I am likely to receive. I challenge them to do better.		
• I lead my people through example and motivation, bringing out the best in them. I do not "manage" them.		
• I try to give my people a vision for the future and the strategies for getting there, then try to ensure that they buy into it.		
• I save myself for the big decisions and delegate the authority for all other decisions to my staff. In no way do I micromanage them.		
• I focus on solutions and do not point fingers.		
• I do not play favorites, and discourage corporate politicians of style but little substance.		
Planning		
• Recognizing that planning is another word for good management, we prepare a detailed business plan with challenging, measurable goals and strategies for achieving those goals.		

	Yes	No
Planning *(con't.)*		
• Specific tasks and responsibilities are established, with target dates.		
• We have distilled our plan into a few key strategic factors, objectives, and methods of implementation that we believe are vital to our future success.		
• The plan was prepared with the full input and support of all staff members important to its execution.		
• The plan is monitored as least quarterly by the CEO.		
• The plan is updated semiannually at a minimum.		
• We have defined what our strengths are and now seek to build on them.		
• Our planning process and brainstorming sessions have been productive and creative, raising important and even unpleasant issues and evaluations we had not been confronting.		
• The plan is used as a means to manage, guide, and grow the business.		
Customers		
• We view each customer as an annuity, providing a continuous stream of revenue, and we do all in our power to maintain that revenue stream.		
• As a small business, we recognize the opportunity and expectation that we differentiate ourselves from our competition through providing personal, caring service.		
• We have an organizationwide commitment that focuses all of the business resources toward our goal of delighting customers.		
• We recognize that the definition of superb service is exceeding our customers' expectations.		
• Our record shows that we have a loyal customer base. (Are you sure about this?)		
• We regularly survey and meet with our customers to ascertain their needs and suggestions, and how responsive we are to them.		

	Yes	No
Customers *(con't.)*		
• We make a point of contacting our former customers to ascertain why they chose our competitors, and we seek to have them do business with us again.		
• We try to "customerize" our service and meet special requests or requirements.		
• We recognize that our employees are our ambassadors to our customers, thus we treat them as we expect them to treat our customers.		
• We provide ongoing customer service training to our staff, including role playing from the customers' perspective.		
• We have set forth guidelines for good customer service, and we empower our employees to promptly and courteously resolve our customers' problems and complaints.		
• We maintain a list of "problem customers"—those requiring special attention—and we provide it.		
• Our market share is growing.		
• We view each new day as a selling day, and we bring the same intensity and commitment to all customers, old and new. There is no complacency.		
• Our selling, ordering, and distribution systems have been streamlined to further facilitate customer service.		
Financial Plan/Finances		
• We prepare a detailed annual financial plan, including cash flow projections.		
• We recognize that our plan is only as good as the assumptions on which it is based; therefore, we try to make our sales projections as realistic and accurate as possible.		
• We recognize the importance of a financial plan as an indispensable and practical guide to expense and cash control and as a means for monitoring and controlling the business.		
• The financial plan is updated as necessary throughout the year.		

	Yes	No
Financial Plan/Finances ***(con't.)***		
• Our projections are made by product/service line.		
• Monthly performance is compared with forecasts, and our experience in this area is used to prepare more accurate forecasts in subsequent years.		
• Managers are required to account for the variations between actual results and forecasts for their areas of responsibility.		
• We use our plan to project financing needs, to assist in inventory and human resource needs, and as an early warning system for developing possible contingency plans.		
• We have the necessary financial controls in place with which to manage the business—for example, budgets, cash flow forecasts, costing systems, and timely, accurate, and relevant financial statements.		
• Detailed financial and cash flow statements, with budgetary comparisons, are prepared by the 15th of the following month and are shared to the extent necessary with those in positions of responsibility.		
• Full accrual accounting is used in preparing the financial statements.		
• Full reserve is made on the monthly financial statements for bad debts and obsolete inventory.		
• The inventory count agrees with the balance sheet figure.		
• The financial statements are understood by management and are utilized as a means to manage and direct the business.		
• Our financial reports evaluate the profitability of each product/service line and provide relevant data on all of our operating and selling costs.		
• Our CFO can be considered a financial manager, one who can read the big picture and link the business's financial performance with its objectives.		

	Yes	No
Expense Control		
• We apply the question "If we eliminate this expense, will we lose revenue?" to all expenditures.		
• If the answer is no, then we eliminate the expense.		
• We recognize that lower costs lead to lower prices, which in turn leads to greater volume. This leads to lower costs, which perpetuates the cycle.		
• All expenses contribute to and translate into improved quality and customer satisfaction.		
• There are no unjustified expenses. (If you answer yes to this question, award yourself the Nobel Prize for Expense Control and call the King of Sweden to schedule the award ceremony.)		
• Our philosophy is "Price – Cost = Profit" rather than "Cost + Profit = Price."		
• We have eliminated duplication of effort, busywork, unnecessary procedures, paperwork, and bottlenecks.		
• Our organization has no sacred cows—untouchable staff, procedures, or methods—that may be burdening our overhead. Everything and everybody comes under review.		
• We do not "hire somebody" every time a difficulty arises.		
• We carry only the minimum of "non–revenue producing" individuals, and there is no middle or upper management bureaucratic fat. (Are you sure about this?)		
• Our sales commissions are structured to be based on the profit margin and the degree of difficulty involved in making the sale.		
• We recognize that expense management is essential in both good times and bad.		
• In reducing expenses, we are careful not to cut muscle along with fat.		
• We periodically conduct an organizational analysis and do not have more than four staff levels, including the CEO.		
• The CEO and senior managers each have from seven to ten individuals reporting to them.		

	Yes	No
Expense Control *(con't.)*		
• We annually conduct a ratio analysis based on data from the last five years. Any aberrant figures are investigated further.		
• We have a quality improvement program in place.		
• We have established an ABC purchasing prioritizing system to better focus our efforts on achieving maximum savings.		
• We have established a specific cost reduction percentage for our purchasing department to achieve and provide the necessary support to them in that endeavor.		
• Every supplier's price increase automatically triggers a competitive bidding situation.		
• We are careful not to lock ourselves into one supplier for any product, unless we do so as the result of a competitive bidding process.		
• We reward our employees for increasing their productivity.		
• We maximize efficiency with employee cross-training programs.		
• We are utilizing the latest time, cost, or energy-saving devices or systems for our industry.		
• Our cost accounting system identifies unprofitable products and business segments.		
• We have a cost system in place that provides accurate information on our costs by product/service.		
• Our expense ratios compare favorably with the norms for our industry.		
Pricing for Profit		
• Through market research and price experimentation, we seek to establish the optimum price for our product or service.		
• We monitor our price levels on an ongoing basis.		
• We seek to establish our prices at the level that will yield the largest total profit flow.		

	Yes	No
Pricing for Profit *(con't.)*		
• We pursue a specific pricing strategy that is linked to our overall pricing objective.		
• We know our precise costs by product and utilize this information to establish our prices.		
• We know our break-even point on all products/services at varying price levels.		
• We carefully consider the impact of our pricing decisions on profitability.		
• Our marketing/sales staff consult with management in establishing prices; however, the final decision on pricing rests with management.		
• We recognize the vital importance of unit sales volume to the maintenance of reasonable price levels.		
• We recognize that an expense reduction of the same percentage can be as beneficial to profitability as a price increase.		
• We realize that in raising prices, we may lose demand or customers. We therefore conduct adequate research, provide advance notification, and try to provide a value-added benefit in support of any increase.		
• Recognizing that 80% of profit usually comes from 20% of the business, we continually review and allocate resources and marketing efforts accordingly.		
Cash Flow		
• We have sufficient working capital available for our short-term and long-term needs.		
• The need for cash consciousness plays a large part in decision making at all levels of the business.		
• As suppliers and payroll are paid from cash flow, not profits, we recognize the need for an adequate cash flow in managing the business.		
• Our line of credit is sufficient for our needs.		

	Yes	No
Cash Flow *(con't.)*		
• We have a strict credit management program that we adhere to.		
• Our CEO and CFO carefully review our aged accounts receivables detail semimonthly.		
• Our accounts receivable average days of sales outstanding (DSO) is less than the norm for our industry.		
• Our bad debts write-off percentage is less than the norm for our industry.		
• We take advantage of prompt payment discounts and other incentives.		
• We recognize profit as an accounting concept, while cash flow is an operating concept. We recognize that the two do not necessarily go hand-in-hand.		
• Recognizing the importance of cash flow, we are wary of overtrading and try to have controlled rather than rapid growth, which might overextend our resources.		
• We recognize that cash flow problems can drown a successful business in its own prosperity.		
• We do not allow ourselves to overextend credit and play the role of banker for our customers.		
• We do not allow our sales policy to influence our credit policy.		
• We perform credit checks on all new customers and annual credit checks on those customers that account for 80% of our business.		
• We set credit limits on each account, and our sales staffs are informed when a customer is at or near that limit.		
• Our credit manager's decision can only be overruled by the CEO or CFO.		
• We pay strict attention to invoicing to eliminate billing lags; we try to deliver invoices with goods or immediately thereafter.		
• We are quick to spot any deviations in customer payment patterns and red flag them as necessary.		

	Yes	No
Cash Flow *(con't.)*		
• Our inventory turnover rates exceed the norms for our industry.		
• Recognizing the true cost of carrying inventory, we have a system in place to keep it moving and to prevent obsolescence.		
• We have an order entry system that matches orders, inventory, and production schedules by product code.		
• Our inventory levels are less than the norm for our industry.		
Prosperity and Failure		
• We do not pursue short-term profitability at the expense of long-term competitive strength.		
• We recognize that good performance frequently results from a combination of agressive marketing, investment support, increased spending on product development, improved quality, and new product introductions.		
• We recognize our marketing expenditures as investments that drive revenue over time and maintain them during both good and bad times.		
• I am not a "boss-autocrat," engaged in one-man rule.		
• I recognize that my position requires me to be a good delegator and motivator.		
• Failure as well as success start at the top. Therefore, when there are shortcomings with the business I look at myself first, since the business reflects me and is an extension of me.		
• Our profitability matches or exceeds the norm for our industry.		
• The "Peter principle" does not apply to any key staff members.		
• We are wary of overdiversification and try to stick to our core business and competencies.		

	Yes	No
Prosperity and Failure *(con't.)*		
• We recognize that the marketplace is dynamic and ever-changing, and that there is no room for complacency if we do not want to be swept aside.		
• Rather than depend on one large customer, we try to maintain a broad customer base to limit the impact of any customer losses.		
• Our products are not being rendered obsolete by changes in the marketplace.		
Management		
• We place strong emphasis on managing for the long term, and pay particular attention to developing our invisible assets: market share/position, product quality, distribution system, our people, customer base, and the equity in our name.		
• Our control system monitors the key indicators: cash on hand, receivables, inventory, sales, expenses, payroll, gross profit ratios, operating profit, marketing results, sales volume, turnaround time, revenue, and profits per employee.		
• We create an innovative climate conducive to fostering creativity and generating new ideas.		
• We have the necessary resources in terms of cash, equipment, and qualified staff to successfully grow the business.		
• A clear business strategy is reflected in all decisions concerning new markets, new business, or new products.		
• Our concept of business-as-usual is one of dynamism and commitment to continuous improvement in all areas.		
• Management decisions are followed through to a successful conclusion.		
• Management control is exercised through motivation rather than regulation.		

	Yes	No
Management *(con't.)*		
• We do not have an autocratic, military-style chain of command that stifles initiative, the freedom to speak, and the depth of employee commitment.		
• We are not averse to bringing in new blood from the outside if we feel it is necessary.		
• Our performance would not be enhanced by replacing certain individuals.		
• Management is deeply involved with the business's operations at all times.		
• Management continually interacts with employees at all levels.		
• We have a profit-sharing plan that is open to all.		
• When I see or am presented with a good idea, I act on it.		
• We are fully abreast of all technological changes that can affect our industry.		
• We have a keen understanding of the trends in our industry and have made plans to deal with them.		
• We actively get out into the marketplace to measure its pulse.		
• We are quick to admit a problem or perceive a changing marketplace and take the necessary corrective action.		
• As a leader, I am not averse to delegating authority and giving others the opportunity to make decisions and grow.		
• We invest in the future.		

Index

A

A-B-C purchasing classes, 30
Accounting systems, need for, 20, 124
Accounts payable, 60
Accounts receivable
  cash flow and, 41–46, 49–54
  as key indicator, 128
  management of, 51–54
ACE staff members, 3–4
Added value, 89
Advertising, 117–18, 129
Annuity value
  of customers, 85, 86
  of intangible assets, 115
Assets
  customers as, 85
  intangible, 114–16, 133
  inventory as, 55–56
  sale and leaseback of, 60
Assurance, in service, 93
Attitude, of staff, 3
Autocratic rule, 119–20
Avis, Warren, 14

B

Balance sheet
  components of, 114
  intangible, 114–16
Bere, James T., 120
Billing system, 54–55. *See also* Accounts receivable; Invoicing
Bonuses, 10
Borg-Warner Corporation, 120
Break-even analysis, 68, 69
Budgets, 34, 124. *See also* Expenses
Bureaucratic jobs, 18
Business planning, 101–12
  benefits of, 103–4
  checkup questions about, 136–37
  employee involvement in, 103–6
  failure of, 111
  goals in, 107–8
  objectives in, 108–10, 111
  participatory nature of, 103, 105
  questions addressed by, 106–7
  steps in, 104–10
  updating of, 110, 111
Buzzell, Robert, 117

C
Capitalization, 37
Cash flow, 37–61
accounts receivable and, 41–46, 49–54
checkup questions about, 142–44
compared to profit, 37–45
credit management and, 49–55
factors affecting, 48
formula for, 48
growth and, 39–48
inventory and, 41–46, 55–60
Cash flow cycle, 38
Cash flow forecasting, 38, 46, 124
Cash on hand, 127–28
CEO (chief executive officer), 18, 21–22, 119–20
CFO (chief financial officer), 124, 127
Change
adapting to, 121, 125
in the marketplace, 121, 125–26
resistance to, 17, 36, 111
Character, of staff, 3
Cheerleaders, managers as, 120
Chief executive officer (CEO), 18, 21–22, 119–20
Chief financial officer (CFO), 124, 127
Chrysler, 120
Chussil, Mark J., 117
Coaches, managers as, 120
Cold calling, 97
Collection, 49, 51–54
Compensation plans. *See also* Payroll
investment in, 2
leadership and, 10
sales commissions in, 19–20
staff management and, 7
Competitors
complacency and, 121, 133
customers of, 91, 92
pricing and, 63–65, 73–77, 79
Complacency, 121, 133
Computerized systems, 59
Conformists, 4
Connor, Denis, 2
Consistency, and leadership, 10
Control and reporting system, 127
Conversion
of inquiries into sales, 129
of variable costs into fixed costs, 15
Corporate culture, 4–5
customer service and, 88, 91–96
innovation in, 131–32
planning and, 111
Cost-based pricing, 64
Costing systems, 124
Cost-plus pricing, 15, 63
Costs
of carrying inventory, 55–56
knowledge of, 83
of poor service, 90–91
pricing and, 15, 66–69, 74, 82, 83
of recruiting customers, 116
reduction of, 13–36
Creativity, 4, 5, 105, 131–32
Credit management, 49–55
Culture. *See* Corporate culture
Customer audits, 91–92
Customer base
as intangible asset, 114
limited, 123–24
Customerized service, 93
Customers
annuity value of, 85, 86
checkup questions about, 137–38

Customers—*continued*
delighting of, 86, 89
employees as, 94
feedback from, 88, 91–93, 96–97, 98
loyalty of, 88, 89
pricing and, 14, 72–73, 76, 79, 81
recruiting vs. retention of, 116
Customer service, 86–100
characteristics of, 92–93
culture of, 88, 91–96
employee satisfaction and, 93–96
poor, cost of, 90–91
salesmanship as, 87
superb, 89, 91–93

D
Data. *See also* Key indicators
financial, 124
for ratio analysis, 22–25
Days of sales outstanding (DSO), 50, 128
Days on hand, of inventory, 128
Determination, of staff, 3
Distribution system, 114
Diversification, over-, 123
Downsizing, 18–19
Drucker, Peter, 103
DSO (days of sales outstanding), 50, 128

E
Ego, of CEO, 119–20
Employees. *See also* Corporate culture
ACE qualities of, 3–4
business planning by, 103–6
checkup questions about, 135–36
as customers, 94
customer service and, 88, 93–96
empowerment of, 6, 94–95, 120, 132
frontline, 94, 95
hiring of, 1–12
as intangible asset, 114
leadership of, 8–12
levels of, 18, 21–22, 29
management of, 5–8
nonproductive, 17–19
Peter Principle on, 125
in successful businesses, 117–18
Employee satisfaction, 93–96
Empowerment, 6, 94–95, 120, 132
Enthusiasm, 3, 11
Environment, employee, 6, 9, 11. *See also* Corporate culture
Equity, in name, 114
Expansion, 122. *See also* Growth
Expenses
cash flow and, 60
checkup questions about, 140–41
efficient use of, 21
interest, and accounts receivable, 50
as key indicator, 128
management of, 20–21
reduction of, 13–36
review of, 32–36

F
Failure
in business planning, 111
causes of, 119–26
checkup questions about, 144–45
Finances. *See also* Expenses
checkup questions about, 138–39
controls on, 124–25
data on, 124
Financial planning, 34, 138–39

Financial statements, 68, 124
Fixed costs, 15
Focus groups, 97
Freedom, of employees, 5
Frontline employees, 94, 95

G
Gates, Bill, 2
General Motors, 121
Goals, in planning, 107–8
Gross profit ratios, 129
Growth
- cash flow and, 39–48
- liquidity crisis in, 122
- management skills needed for, 113–14
- personal and business, 2
- planning for, 102

H
Hiring, 1–12

I
Iacocca, Lee, 120
IBM, 121
Income statement, 68
Incremental cost pricing, 82
Indicators, key, 127–31. *See also* Ratio analysis
Innovation, 121, 131–32
Inquiries, and marketing, 129
Intangible assets, 114–16, 133
Interest expense, 50
Inventory. *See also* Purchasing
- cash flow and, 41–46, 55–60
- management of, 56–60
- sales and, 128
- turnover of, 56–57, 128
- vendor stocking and, 31

Investment, 2, 117–18
Invoicing, 53. *See also* Billing system

K
Key indicators, 127–31. *See also* Ratio analysis
Key strategic factors, 108–10
KMart, 16

L
Labor cost, 66–67
Leadership, 8–12
- effective, 9–11
- ineffective, 120
- in planning, 111
- ultimate task of, 11
Leaseback, 60
Letter of credit, 60
Lincoln, Abraham, 120
Liquidity crisis, 122
Listening
- to customers, 88, 91–93, 96–97, 98
- to employees, 11

M
Management
- checkup questions on, 145–46
- of employees, 5–8
- importance of, 113–33
- innovation and, 131–32
- intangible assets and, 114–16
- micro-, 7–8, 119
- in problem businesses, 119–26
- in successful businesses, 117–18
Management information systems, 127. *See also* Data; Key indicators
Managers, in organizational structure, 18, 21–22

Marketing
importance of, 117–18
results of, 129
Marketplace, changing, 121, 125–26
Market share, 114, 126
Marshall, George C., 7
Materials. *See* Purchasing
Mentors, managers as, 120
Micromanagement, 7–8, 119
Microsoft, 74
Morale, 2
Motivation, 1, 10, 11, 19, 20
Mystery customers, 97

N
Name, equity in, 114
Napoleon, 2
Nonconformists, 4

O
Objectives, in planning, 108–10, 111
One-man rule, 119–20
One-price policy, 83
Operating profit
as key indicator, 129
pricing and, 66–81
Order entry system, 60
Orders, turnaround time for, 130
Organizational analysis, 18, 21–22
Organization chart
flatness of, 18
staff levels in, 18, 21–22, 29
Overdiversification, 123
Overhead
control of, 13, 14
pricing and, 66–68, 69
Overtime, 19

P
Payables, 60
Payroll. *See also* Compensation plans
cash flow and, 60
excessive staff and, 17
as key indicator, 129
trimming of, 27
Penetration pricing, 65
People. *See* Employees
Perot, Ross, 2, 3
Persistence, of staff, 3
Peter, Lawrence, 125
Peter Principle, 125
Planning. *See* Business planning; Financial planning
Plant cost, 67
Positions, evaluation of, 18, 33
Predatory pricing, 65
Premium pricing, 71–75, 80–81
Prestige pricing, 65
Price decreases, 15–16
analysis of, 75–78
limitations of, 76
Price freezes, 31
Price increases
analysis of, 71–75, 78–79
limitations of, 13–14, 15, 72, 73
Pricing, 63–83
break-even analysis for, 68, 69
changes in, 13–14, 15–16, 69–79
checkup questions about, 141–42
competitors and, 63–65, 73–77, 79
cycle of costs and, 15, 74
product lines and, 79–81
profit formula and, 66–68
sales volume and, 66–68, 69–79
strategies of, 63–65, 82–83
Product cost, 66–68, 69

Productivity, 17–19, 129, 130
Product life cycle, 130
Product lines
key indicators and, 128, 129, 130
pricing and, 79–81
Product portfolio, 114
Product quality, as intangible asset, 114
Profit
checkup questions about, 135–46
compared to cash flow, 37–45
efforts needed for, xi–xii
pricing and, 66–81
turned into losses, 126
Profit formula, 66–68
Profit margin, 66–79, 80
Profit per employee, 130–31
Profit sharing, 7, 10
Promotions
employee, 125
marketing, 118, 129
Prosperity
checkup questions about, 144–45
management in, 117–18
Purchasing, 29–32. *See also* Inventory

Q
Quality
customer service and, 90, 92
expense reduction and, 18, 19, 27–29
as intangible asset, 114
position evaluation and, 18, 19
pricing and, 72, 80, 81

R
Ratio analysis, 22–27. *See also* Key indicators
Receivables. *See* Accounts receivable
Recognition, of employees, 7
Reliability, in service, 92
Reporting system, 127
Resistance to change
in expense reduction, 17, 36
in planning, 111
Resources
for employees, 1
employees as, 1, 87
Responsiveness, in service, 92–93
Revenue per employee, 130–31
Robert Morris and Associates, 130
Russian roulette pricing, 64

S
Sacred cows, and cost control, 16–17
Salary. *See* Compensation plans; Payroll
Sale and leaseback, 60
Sales
cash flow and, 39–48
customer service and, 87, 92
inquiries and, 129
inventory and, 128
as key indicator, 128
Sales commissions, 19–20, 52
Sales force, 117–18
Sales volume
expense reductions and, 36
importance of, 71
as key indicator, 130
pricing and, 66–68, 69–79
Sears, 16, 121
Service, customer. *See* Customer service
Skimming pricing, 64
Small businesses, customer service by, 87

Software, for inventory management, 59
Southwest Airlines, 74
Staff, ACE qualities of, 3–4. *See also* Employees
Stock purchase plans, 7
Strategic factors, 108–10
Strategy objectives, 108–10
Success
  characteristics of, 117–18
  checkup questions about, 144–45
Suppliers
  expense reduction and, 30–32
  inventory management and, 59
Surveys, 96–97

T
Tactical objectives, 109
Target dates, 109–10
Target pricing, 64
Teams, 6
Toll-free numbers, 97
Total quality management (TQM), 28, 29
Training, for customer service, 94
Treasure hunters, 116
Truman, Harry S., 10
Turnaround time, 130
Turnover, inventory, 56–57, 128

U
Undercapitalization, 122
Unit sales price, 66–67

V
Value, 81, 89. *See also* Quality
Variable costs, 15, 66–68, 69
Vendors. *See* Suppliers
Vendor stocking, 31
Vision, shared, 103, 105

W
Wal-Mart, 7, 15–16, 95–96
Walton, Sam, 2, 9, 95–96
Warmth, in service, 93

About the Author

Richard Peelo is the president of Profit Dynamics, Inc., a business advisory service. The firm specializes in improving the profitability of small to midsize businesses through cost containment, revenue enhancement, improved pricing, strategy development, employee selection, and focus on the customer.

If you hire speakers for your company, or influence the choice of speakers for your trade association, please contact us to learn more about how we can help you, your company, or your membership multiply your profits.

We are always happy to discuss the individual criteria of each company or group, and how we may tailor a program to your specific requirements.

To learn more about how Profit Dynamics, Inc. can help you multiply your profits, contact Richard Peelo at

Profit Dynamics, Inc.
137 South Roberts
Inverness, IL 60067-4547
Phone 847-202-1500 Fax 847-202-1502
E-mail bldprofits@aol.com